ROYAL MARYS

" THE LADY MARY TUDOR " (QUEEN MARY I).
From a picture in the Ashmolean Museum.

[Frontispiece

ROYAL MARYS

PRINCESS MARY AND HER PREDECESSORS

BY E. THORNTON COOK

AUTHOR OF "HER MAJESTY : THE ROMANCE OF THE QUEENS
OF ENGLAND," "THEIR MAJESTIES OF SCOTLAND," AND
"ROYAL ELIZABETHS"

Essay Index Reprint Series

BOOKS FOR LIBRARIES PRESS, INC.

FREEPORT, NEW YORK

First published 1930
Reprinted 1967

PRINTED IN THE UNITED STATES OF AMERICA

DEDICATED BY GRACIOUS PERMISSION TO THE
" ROYAL MARY " OF THE PRESENT GENERA-
TION, HER ROYAL HIGHNESS PRINCESS MARY
COUNTESS OF HAREWOOD

INTRODUCTION

FOR nearly a thousand years, ever since the daughters of St. Margaret of Scotland fled south to find a temporary refuge in a Hampshire Convent, the name " Mary " has appeared and re-appeared in the annals of our royal line ; curiously often the " Princess Mary " of the day has had a sister Elizabeth.

Some of these princesses have been " ladies of great beautie and eminent virtue," others, " discreet and debonair." Hardly one but has lived romantic days and shown both character and courage.

A " Royal Mary " of the thirteenth century who took the veil in childhood developed into an " attorney " and coped with business matters as competently as any modern maid. One went, weeping, to be a Queen of France, but only on conditions. " Next time " she was to marry " as me liketh ! " Two wedded in Holland, two ruled England—but only one gave us a King.

E. T. C.

"What's past is Prologue."

CONTENTS

xi

CONTENTS xiii

LIST OF ILLUSTRATIONS

CHAPTER I
KINGS' DAUGHTERS
1085 (?)–1181

MARY (OF THE LINE OF ATHOLL)

Born . . . about 1085
Married . . . „ 1102
Died . . . „ ?

Issue : one daughter.

MARY (OF BOULOGNE)

Born 1136
Married 1160
Died 1181

Issue : two daughters.

Descent

Malcolm III, King of Scots, *m.* St. Margaret
|
Mary (line of Atholl) and others
m. Count of Boulogne
|
Matilda
m. King Stephen
|
Mary (of Boulogne) and others
m. Matthew of Flanders

CHAPTER I

KINGS' DAUGHTERS

THE first King's daughter to bear the name of Mary was Scottish born. Her mother was the St. Margaret who, en route from England to Hungary, was driven by stress of weather on to the Fife coast, where Malcolm Canmore fell in love with her at first sight.

Margaret, dreaming of a quiet convent in her native land, had no wish to wed this turbulent Scot, but found that " his love was not to be withstood," so married him and was carried off for a honeymoon at Dunfermline-in-the-Woods, a place " so strongly fortified that neither man nor beast might tread its trackless paths." [1] In the succeeding years she earned admission to the Calendar of Saints.

When King Malcolm and his eldest son were killed in battle Margaret died, and her children were taken to England for safety's

[1] See *Their Majesties of Scotland*, by E. Thornton Cook (Murray).

3

sake, Scotland being in a state of civil war. The two girls, Mary and her elder sister Matilda, were placed in a Hampshire convent where an Abbess aunt welcomed her dead sister's children and undertook their instruction " in the art of reading and the observance of good manners."

In addition the worthy Abbess did her best to persuade her charges to take the vows, but neither had inherited their mother's desire for a religious life, and when, after seven years of rebellion against the authority of this aunt, an opportunity of freedom was offered to the elder princess, she seized it boldly, defied the Abbess and went to share the throne with Henry I.[1]

As a Queen's sister the Lady Mary became politically valuable, so soon she too was able to cast aside the enshrouding veil, which she had worn by compulsion, and marry the Count of Boulogne.

Both sisters had daughters and both christened them Matilda. The Queen's child married Henry V and became an Empress ; Mary's daughter being heiress to Boulogne on the death of her parents was " by the King's means purchased and got in marriage " by Stephen de Blois who,

[1] See *Her Majesty : The Romance of the Queens of England*, by E. Thornton Cook (Murray).

on the death of his uncle Henry I, seized the throne of England and was crowned with his consort Matilda of Boulogne.

TWELFTH CENTURY

King Stephen and Queen Matilda had three children, Eustace, William and Mary, and had modern laws of inheritance been in force this little Princess might well have become our first Queen Regnant. As it was she was sent as a thank-offering to take the veil at the convent where her grandmother and great-aunt had found refuge in their girlhood. And for a space the world forgot her.

England was war-riven while Stephen and his Queen fought to hold the crown claimed by Empress Matilda till, when left to carry on the struggle single handed, Stephen purchased peace by accepting the disinheritance of his own sons and recognising Henry Plantagenet as his successor. Eustace died of rage and William retired to his mother's domain of Boulogne. His death left the country without a ruler, and the people fearing absorption by Henry Plantagenet remembered Mary peacefully praying in her convent.

In the brave days of old might was right

and a woman's dignities fell to her husband without question, so, to aspiring landless knights, Mary, heiress of Boulogne, seemed a glittering prize ; no convent wall was high enough to guard her.

" In that same year Matthew, sonne to the Earle of Flanders, married Ladie Mary the Abbess of Ramsie, daughter to King Stephen and with her had the countie of Bullonge. About this grew the first falling out between King Henry and Chancellor Thomas Becket as some have written ; the Chancellor was sorre against the contract." [1]

Matthew had swooped down upon the convent and risked his immortal soul by carrying off the startled nun-princess who had been immured within its walls since childhood. By this coup he became Count of Boulogne. What were his dreams ? From the same stepping-stone Stephen de Blois had mounted the throne of England and Abbess Mary was Stephen's sole surviving heir.

But Henry II held the sceptre in strong grasp and Matthew was busy in other spheres while Mary gave him two daughters. Then the blow fell. Who knows the reason ? Perhaps an enemy moved, perchance

---

[1] This is a quotation from Holinshed who uses the word " earle."

Matthew, now well established, realised the lack of further usefulness in this wife whose inheritance and children he held.

After ten years' consideration the Church realised the enormity of that long past crime and thundered its curses—they fell upon the weaker vessel and there is no hint in history that Matthew was stirred to a further risking of his soul by intervening.

How dared this woman who had vowed herself to God become wife to mortal man ?

Decree was pronounced. Mary must leave the world, her husband and her children and do penance in her violated convent.

She obeyed. Perhaps she was glad to go. Matthew remained Count of Boulogne and thoughtfully rendered Mary's children legitimate ; when he died the elder succeeded him, while for twelve years Mary offered up her prayers behind the convent walls.

CHAPTER II

THREE EDWARDIAN MARYS

1279–1482

(1) A PORTIA OF THE THIRTEENTH CENTURY :
MARY DAUGHTER OF EDWARD I AND
ELEANORA OF CASTILE.

(2) NURSERY ESPOUSALS : MARY DUCHESS OF
BRITTANY, DAUGHTER OF EDWARD III
AND PHILIPPA OF HAINAULT.

(3) ELIZABETH'S UNDERSTUDY : MARY
DAUGHTER OF EDWARD IV AND
ELIZABETH WOODVILLE.

MARY PLANTAGENET

Born at Windsor   .   .   1279
Entered a Convent .   .   1285
Died   1333

Descent : Sixth daughter of Edward I and Eleanora of Castile.

MARY (DUCHESS OF BRITTANY)

Born at Waltham   .   .   1344
Married John of Montfort .   1361
Died   1361

Descent : Fourth daughter of Edward III and Philippa of Hainault.

MARY (OF YORK)

Born at Windsor   .   .   1466
Died   1482

Descent : Second daughter of Edward IV and Elizabeth Woodville.

CHAPTER II

A PORTIA OF THE THIRTEENTH CENTURY

(MARY PLANTAGENET)

THIRTEENTH CENTURY

NEWS of the birth of a sixth daughter reached Edward I when he was exulting in a martial victory and he quickly decided that the child should become a nun. But Queen Eleanora had no wish to be deprived of one of her children (she was ultimately the mother of nine daughters, including one set of twins), and it was not until Mary was six years old and the Church frowned, asking "how the Queen dared withhold from Heaven this chosen lamb from her numerous flock," that Eleanora acquiesced.

The famous convent of Fontevraud had hoped to receive the King's daughter, but his mother, Eleanor of Provence, had decided to take the veil at Amesbury, so Mary also entered the branch house, Fontevraud being placated by the hint that the little Princess might be sent there later.

All the royal family down to the last baby went to see the six-year-old child take her first vows. The Virgin Mary was selected as her especial patroness and thirteen high-born children of an age to make them suitable playmates for the Lady Mary took the veil with her.

Each white-robed little maiden received a gold ring set with sapphires from the hand of the King.

Mary was dowered with a hundred pounds a year for her expenses and had a dress allowance in addition, while by special decree Southampton was called upon to supply "oil for her lamp and wine for her table."

When the Queen Mother and the Queen-Consort died within a short interval of one another the French convent renewed its plea for the Lady Mary, but she remained on in England, though State papers now referred to her as "the King's dearest daughter, a nun of Fontevraud staying at Amesbury."

But though a nun Mary was not shut away from the world and invariably joined her brothers and sisters for any special festivity.

She wore black serge and a long black veil, as did the other nuns, but was allowed "a gold clasp" as an insignia of rank, and her "cell was luxurious with hangings of velvet and tapestry." She had " cushions on her benches " and " the best linen obtainable," and when she went to Court took a more important position than any of her sisters, being allowed a " train of twenty-four horses" as an escort, while they had only eight !

As she grew up Mary's allowance was doubled and her supply of wine increased ; in addition, she received a goodly number of " forth oaks for a fire in her chamber."

The world wondered, when in the twentieth century a woman was called to the Bar. Six hundred years before, fifteen-year-old Lady Mary, King's daughter and nun though she might be, was grappling with legal mysteries.

She was officially appointed " advocate " and bidden to present the case of the English nuns who objected to an appointment made by the French body. The Lady Mary lost the case but showed herself so capable that, despite her youth, she was appointed " attorney " to the Abbess. This brought the convent's revenues under her charge. She learnt to argue questions of pasturage and give orders that " grasping overbearing neighbours must take away their hands from the goods of the Lady Abbess."

Sometimes it was necessary to appeal to the King's authority and then Mary would

end her official letters on a personal note
that must have been irresistible :

" Do as much, sweet Father, for the love
of me that my Lady Abbess of Fontevraud
may perceive in all things that I am a good
attorney for her in this country ! . . . I commend to Jesus the soul and body of you. . . ."

But if Mary managed the convent's affairs
well she proved a careless financier in personal matters and often found it impossible
to pay her bills. At least one unfortunate
creditor who had supplied her with goods
could not get his just dues and was ultimately
himself imprisoned for debt. He petitioned
the King, pointing out that it was owing to
the royal nun's neglect that he was brought
to this predicament ; Edward paid his
daughter's bills and, so that the scandal
might not occur again, increased her allowance, gave her more wine and more oaks—
yet still Mary's debts accumulated and presently a special grant was required to pay
them, for, alas, nun, princess and capable
attorney, Mary could not refrain from gam-
bling !

She " diced " so frequently when travelling about the country acting as deputy for
the Abbess and settling difficult questions
in connection with various convents, that

she was frequently driven to borrow from her
attendants in order to settle her debts of
honour !

But though business matters claimed
Mary's attention she did not neglect family
affairs. When Edward I married again
Mary gave a friendly welcome to the shy
French Princess, Marguerite,[1] who was some
three years younger than herself, and attended Court to witness the birth of her
stepmother's second child, taking the Queen
on a pilgrimage of thanksgiving afterwards.
The two were often together while Edward
was making war on Scotland until Marguerite
persuaded the King to let her accompany
him on his military excursions. To console
herself for the loss of the Queen's society
Mary went on a round of visits to the most
famous shrines, escorted by an almost royal
train of attendants and minstrels. Her
" dicings " reached such a pitch that " bor-
rowings " from the King became a matter of
urgency.

When Edward I died and Edward II
came to the throne Mary lost none of her
importance. She was called upon to meet
" Isabella the Fair "[1] when her brother

---

[1] For the stories of Marguerite and Isabella see *Her
Majesty : The Romance of the Queens of England*, by
E. Thornton Cook (Murray).

brought his bride from France and became
as firm friends with the new Queen as she
had been with Marguerite.

She still visited at Court and received the
King at her convent, she still went on pil-
grimages, diced and shopped—goods were
cheaper in those days, for she paid " Ròbert
the Draper of St. Albans only 7s. 6d. for thirty
ells of canvas "—and she still applied for
royal backing when necessary although her
letters took on a different tone :

" To the very high and noble prince, her
dear Lord and Brother, Edward by the
Grace of God King of England, his sister
Mary sends health and all manner of reverence," she wrote when on one occasion there
was trouble in the convent, " I pray you . . .
and require you, both for the love of me and
of our convent . . . that you send word to
my Lady Abbess that she do not undertake
to burden our church with any prioress other
than the one we have now. . . . May Jesus
Christ give you a long life, dearest brother. . . ."

When Edward III mounted the throne
after his father's deposition Mary saw to it
that the youthful sovereign confirmed all
the gifts and perquisites that had been
allowed her by his father and grandfather,

indeed she stipulated that her supply of fire-
wood should be increased to " 60 forth oaks."

The last of Mary's numerous band of
brothers and sisters died before Death came
to deliver his summons to her ; she had
been a " nun " for nearly half a century.

NURSERY ESPOUSALS

MARY DUCHESS OF BRITTANY

FOURTEENTH CENTURY

MARY, the fourth daughter of Edward III and Philippa of Hainault (she was known as Mary of Waltham owing to the place of her birth), was born when the uncertain star of her father was temporarily in the ascendant and he had just contrived to redeem his crown from pawn.

The child, one of a band of eleven brothers and sisters, can have seen little of her parents, for Edward III was perpetually in camp and good Queen Philippa as constantly in attendance upon her lord and master. On one occasion at least she, and those of her numerous children who were with her, narrowly escaped capture by the enemy, after which adventure it was considered advisable to leave the younger members of the family in the Tower, or at Woodstock or Eltham, while the parents were on the war-path.

But if times were difficult in England they were still more so in Brittany where

the Duke was a captive in the hands of the
King of France, having sent his little son
John de Montfort to England for safe
keeping. This boy shared the royal children's
nursery while his mother carried on the
fight for her son's inheritance " with the
courage of a man and the heart of a lion."

Mary was born when John was five years
old and for political reasons the children
were espoused when the Duke, having
escaped from captivity, arrived in England
to ask for help. This matter settled, he
returned to help his gallant wife, but news
soon reached England that " death had
clenched his teeth," so Mary, aged one,
became Duchess of Brittany.

Being thus " ranged," the little Princess
slipped into the background leading a quiet
life with her favourite sister Margaret, while
the young Duke waited impatiently till
he should be old enough to strike a blow
for his inheritance. Mary and Margaret
were too young to know that the fortune
of war had forced them into political rivalry.

A lucky stroke had delivered the Duke's
enemy Charles of Blois into Edward's hand,
and Charles, tiring of imprisonment in the
Tower, presently offered a tempting sum for
ransom and suggested himself as a suitable
husband for Margaret.

Edward, in dire straits for money as usual, temporised. He accepted Charles' children as hostages in their father's stead and permitted his prisoner to return to France to see what could be arranged. Then conscience won the day and Edward was forced to realise that the freeing of Charles would be an act of treachery towards John de Montfort, Duke of Brittany, and that Margaret's marriage to Charles would necessitate the breaking of the contract between Mary and John.

When Charles returned with a dispensation for the marriage and full money-bags he found the tide against him and had to go back to the Tower while the young Duke rode at the King's side in a tournament.

All innocently the little sisters played together, visited certain noble houses and spent their meagre allowance of "twenty marks" apiece, till the Duke of Brittany made his first bold attempt to win back his lost lands—and failed. He returned to England to prepare for a second effort and in the interval married Mary.

He was twenty, she seventeen and she went to her wedding in "cloth of gold of Lucca furred and turned up with ermine."

Margaret was married almost at the same

time and within a very few weeks both
sisters died. They were buried together
while the bereaved bridegrooms took solemn
oath " never to marry again—at least without the King's consent." . . . (The Duke
of Brittany was to take unto himself two
more brides !)

ELIZABETH'S UNDERSTUDY

MARY OF YORK

MARY of York, daughter of the unpopular Queen known as " the widow-woman of England,"[1] was born sixteen months after her elder sister Elizabeth and her birth caused an outbreak of dismay. One daughter had been welcome, a second seemed a grave mistake, for the King and the nation required a prince. However, the Archbishop of Canterbury was one of her sponsors and the Queen was granted an allowance of £400 a year on which to bring up her two daughters.

When the King made his will before departing to carry on the war in France he so far forgave Mary her sex that he left her an equal portion with her elder sister :

" Item, we wil that owre doughtre Elizabeth have X M marč towards her marriage, and that owre daughtre Marie

---

[1] See Elizabeth Woodville in *Her Majesty : The Romance of the Queens of England,* by E. Thornton Cook.

22

have also to her marriage X M marč so that
they may be gouverned and ruled in their
marriages by our dearest wife the Queen,
and by our said son the Prince if God
fortunes him to come to years of discretion."

If either of the daughters married without
the necessary consent " which God forbid ! "
she, " so marrying herself " should have
" noo payment of the said X M marč."

Yes, Mary had her uses, for when peace
was made with France and as one of the
conditions the Dauphin was betrothed to
Elizabeth, Edward IV was able to insert
his second daughter's name as a substitute
for Elizabeth so that the connection he
desired should not be lost in the event of
Elizabeth's untimely death.

But when Mary was about sixteen a
tentative offer was made for her hand.
She was to have first place in a marriage
contract—not as a possible understudy for
the part Elizabeth was desired to play—
and the proposed bridegroom was a reigning
monarch—the ten-year-old King of Denmark.

Mary's upbringing had not prepared her
to play a prominent part and " she deceased
before the consummation thereof on the
Thursday before Whitsunday." Mary died
at Greenwich but she was carried to Windsor
to be buried. " Several lords and ladies

were present when her dirge was sung "
and " on the morrow she had her masses."

Had the little Princess lived longer she
would have been driven into sanctuary with
her mother and sisters and have shared in
the agony of uncertainty that hung over
them when rumour had it that the little
Princes, Mary's brothers, had been done
to death in the Tower.

CHAPTER III

"MARYE THE FRENCHE QUENE"

1496–1533

MARY TUDOR

Born (at Richmond) . .	March 1, 1496
Married (at St. Denys) .	October 9, 1514
Crowned Queen of France .	November 5, 1514
Widowed . . .	January 1, 1515
Re-married . . .	May 13, 1515
Died	June 23/4, 1533

Descent

Henry VII *m.* Elizabeth of York

|

Mary (and others)
m. (1) Louis XII of France,
(2) Charles Brandon, Duke of Suffolk

Issue : one son and two daughters by the second husband.
The daughters survived their mother.

CHAPTER III

"MARYE THE FRENCHE QUENE"

FIFTEENTH–SIXTEENTH CENTURIES

MARY TUDOR, who was christened most probably after her mother's sister,[1] was several years younger than the next member of the family who later became Henry VIII, and was handed over to the care of " moder Guilford " as she soon learned to call Lady Guildford. In addition she had a nurse at 50s. a quarter, and, being a delicate child, a special physician who dosed her well on 25s. a day.

By the time Mary was four years old she showed budding promise of becoming " the fairest princess in Europe." She was established in a nursery at Eltham with her own staff, including a wardrobe-keeper and a schoolmaster, for lessons had begun, and the child was studying Latin and French as well as music, dancing and embroidery.

In Queen Elizabeth's carefully kept accounts there are various items concerning

[1] See previous chapter, " Elizabeth's Understudy."

27

her little daughter, 20*d*. to a tailor who
made " a gown of blalk satyn for the Ladye
Marye," with " llj for the hemming of her
kirtle " and twopence for the purchase of
" a letter of pardon " which would permit
her to take part in some festival.' But the
Queen died when Mary was seven years old
and lonely Katharine of Aragon, the widow
of Mary's elder brother Prince Arthur, developed a very real friendship for the child
who was left solitary now that her sister
Margaret had been sent to marry a most
unwilling King of Scots.[1]

Two years later matrimonial advances
began for Mary. It was rumoured that
Emanual of Portugal wanted her for his
son, but the first definite offer arrived just
before Mary's twelfth birthday and was
welcomed by Henry since he was desirous
of strengthening the bond between England
and Spain and thought that by betrothing
Mary to Charles, Prince of Castile, grandson
of the Emperor Maximilian, he would arrive
at the same end more easily than by himself
marrying that prince's mentally deranged
mother, as had been suggested.

Charles, two years younger than Mary,
was in the keeping of the Council of Flanders,

[1] See *Their Majesties of Scotland*, by E. Thornton Cook
(Murray).

MARY TUDOR, QUEEN OF FRANCE.

From a picture in the National Gallery.

28]

which body agreed to open preliminary
negotiations at " the Kyngs toune of Calays
. . . so, in October there came out of England the Bishop of Winchester Lord Privy
Seal and other ambassadors, and there
came to Calais out of Flanders various as
ambassadors. The Lieutenant of the Castle
came out to meet them well attended with
all the spears and archers on horseback and
soldiers in harness, for these strangers feared
the Frenchmen, but being brought in safetie
to Calays there the lords of both partyes
concluded the marriage between the Prynce
of Castile, Archduke of Austriye and the
Ladye Marye daughter to Kyng Henry VII."

The " magistracy of the city " was part
of the security offered for the payment of
Mary's dower and it was agreed that deputies
should be sent to England to witness a
proxy marriage after which the bride was to
remain in her own country until Charles'
fourteenth birthday when she was to be
" delivered up " at Helvoet Sluys, the
journey to be made " at the Kyngs charges."

The contracting parties agreed to pay a
heavy fine for breach of agreement though
the treaty was " so surely established and
knit on both parts that it cannot be dissolved
or broken unless by death. . . . And it
is of truth and undoubted that there was

never amity or alliance heretofore made and
concluded betwixt any princes with better
will and mind, without colour of dissimulation than this."

So there was " great triumph made in
Calays " for the " most noble alliance and
greatest marriage in all Christendom," and
Henry, not wishing his virtues to be over-
looked, pointed out that it was by means
of his " great labour, study and policy that
this honourable marriage had been concluded." In his capable hands daughters
became valuable assets.

The conference now transferred itself to
England where " Tharchbysshopee of
Caunterbury, the Bysshop of Wynchester,
th' Erll of Arundell with dyvers and many
great lords " examined the " commyssions
and writings the ambassadors produced for
the corroboracion of the sayd amytie and
mariage," than which " by mannes reason
none can be more desyred to be had."

There was the Emperor's acceptation " of
the said amytie which is as large as can be
thought, under his syne and seale," and
another the prince had " syned jointly with
hym," as well as many other papers, and
for the sake of yet further security " a
number of the Lordes and Tounes under
the obessaunce of the younge prynce bounded

themselves in penalties under theyr synes and seales."

This duly accomplished and the treaty of " perpetual peace " having been signed, all adjourned to Greenwich for the wedding where Lord de Bergues acted as proxy for ten-year-old Charles.

Mary, well trained for the ordeal, recited her oath : " I, Mary . . . take thee Lord Charles to my husband and spouse . . . and to him and to you for him, I promise that henceforward, during my natural life, I will have, hold and repute him as my husband . . . and for this I plight my troth to him and to you for him."

Lord de Bergues slipped the " spousal ring " on to the child's finger and sealed the ceremony with a kiss.

There followed a great banquet to which came " dyvers grete Lordes and valiaunt Knyghtes prepared to jouste." The tournament continued for three days " at a right great cost to the King," and Mary under her new title, accompanied by Katharine of Aragon and " a goodlie number of fayre Ladyes," came to watch.

Every day the " Lordes and Knyghtes had dyversitie and change of appareilles " each richer than the last, and between the events the ambassadors delivered " thre

goodlie and right rich tokens and juells
to the sayde Ladye Marye " together
with a letter from Charles beginning " My
Good Mate, with good grace, and as cor-
dially as I can, I recommend myself to
you. . . ."

An outstanding figure among the other
knights was Charles Brandon, whose father
had been standard-bearer for Henry VII
on Bosworth field ; he seemed taller, stronger
and yet more gallant than any of the
romantic figures surrounding him.

And while the knights ran their courses
lesser lights settled the last details, concerning " the transporting of my Lady the Princess of Castile." She was to have " such
stuff as was needful for her wardrobe, her
bedden and her stable," against the solem-
nisation of her marriage. Her bedchamber
should be " hangit with clothe of gold," and
be furnished with " a large trussing bedde "
with curtains of damask, a carpet, " a fethir-
bedde of fyne downe " with bolster and
pillows, every one of these to be provided
with " pillow-beers of fyne holland, also fyne
shetes and ij pairre of fustians for the said
trussing bedde."

An " honourable aged person " was to be
appointed by the King to act as Mary's

chamberlain and she was also to have an almoner and a confessor " both in one person."

To wear on her marriage day she must have " a crown for her head and a goodlie devise for her neke, also a goodlie girdle of gold . . . and for a change on the next day " a cheyne of gold."

The arranging of these details took so long that Christmas was now approaching and the ambassadors were anxious to return to their own country. " Albeit the Kynges Grace was greatly desirous that they should longer tarry yet he let them go with great and honourable gifts of goodly plate, besyds horses, hobies, hawks, hounds and other goodly pleasures."

And yet, after all, the match did not materialise !

In the spring (1509) Henry VII died and Mary's brother, some five years her senior, came to the throne as Henry VIII. For a time he was too much absorbed in affairs of state, his own matrimonial desires, and in projects for the marrying of his favourite Charles Brandon to Margaret of Savoy, to follow up arrangements made for Mary.

Later it was agreed that the contracting parties should meet before May 1514 for the

further necessary ceremonies, after which
the united countries should make a joint
attack upon France. The arrangement
sounded admirable and Henry ordered more
" grete justes " in honour of the understanding and certain victories.

These " the kyng attended, with XXIIIj
knights in coates of purple velvet and cloth
of gold and Charles Brandon now Viscount
Lisle answering all comers. . . . There were
many speres broken and many a good buffet
geven . . . and when the justes were done
the kyng and all the others unhelmed them
and rode about the tylt doting grte reverence
to the ladyes, and then the heralds cried to
lodging " !

A few months later Charles Brandon was
created Duke of Suffolk ; it was rumoured
that this was to further his suit with Margaret of Savoy, Regent of the Netherlands.
Mary watched him with admiring eyes as he
rode by her brother's side.

And now there were odd whispers about
the Court. It was rumoured that the Emperor Maximilian was negotiating with France
behind Henry's back. Some went so far as
to affirm that he had made a secret treaty
of peace with France and that in this treaty

was a clause arranging for the marriage of Mary's fiancé to a French Princess !

Bluff King Hal could not believe in such perfidy " so sent a message into Flanders that he had made all arrangements for the marriage of his sister." But " the Council of Flanders replied that they would not receive her that year . . . with many subtyl arguments by reason whereof the amity between England and the Low Countries was much slaked."

Henry's wrath knew no bounds and he protested indignantly that he had been put to great expense in the preliminaries essential for the disposing of his sister, while she had treasured a portrait of Charles for years, " sighing for her spouse ten times a day." All to no purpose ; the treaty between Maximilian and Louis was accomplished and Mary Tudor had been jilted.

But before Henry's royal rage could send him to seek vengeance a soothing message arrived from Louis XII. Through the death of Anne of Brittany he had most conveniently become a widower and would himself be glad to marry Mary, provided that his ambassadors were provided with a safe conduct in order that they might treat for the beautiful Princess.

The envoys having arrived, explained that

they understood the projected marriage
between Charles Prince of Castile and the
King's sister had " broken down " ; therefore
they were now free to express their great
desire that she " might be joined in marriage with the French King " who was ready
to offer not only " a great dowrie, but securi-
ties for the same."

There was much to do. A contract had
to be drawn up by which Mary laid aside
the title of Princess of Castile and testified
her unwillingness to go further with the
marriage since she had heard that Charles
had been " inspired with hatred towards
herself."

But she was left little time in which to
dream of freedom or that gallant knight
Charles Brandon, Duke of Suffolk, for on
the very day of the signing of the nullifica-
tion came a formal proposal from " the most
Christian King of France," and Henry,
" moved by the sincere love he bore his
sister," appointed ambassadors to further
negotiations.

When it was found that Louis was prepared to make an annual payment in con-
solidation of that " pension " which had
fallen sadly into arrears, formerly paid by
the Kings of France to the Kings of England
in lieu of rights claimed by the latter in

connection with the French crown, provided that after a proxy marriage Mary should be delivered over in Abbeville " at her brother's expense," Henry accepted the offer and ordered the drafting of an explanatory letter to the Pope. It was necessary to clear himself of any suspicion of being a breaker of treaties.

Briefly he explained how, although he had carried out every obligation, the guardians of the Prince of Castile had failed to complete arrangements, whereupon he, Henry, " after divers consultations with discreet persons had determined to decree as null and void that which has been contracted by his late father in Mary's name."

Of necessity he admitted that he had now " been alloured to give consent " to his sister's marriage with the King of France in the hope that such marriage " would bring peace to the whole Christian Commonwealth."

There was need to act swiftly for Louis was old and worn for his fifty-two years, but eighteen-year-old Mary was not a Tudor for nothing. She extracted " conditions " before she yielded and stipulated that " next time " she must be left free " to marry as me liketh."

So the treaty was signed " and two men

on horseback rode through London streets
proclaiming peace with France but few took
notice."

Prisoners of war now in England then
" paid their ransoms," among them the
Duke de Longueville who undertook the
office of proxy bridegroom.

A week later a very similar ceremony to
that in which Mary had taken part in her
childhood, when the Lord de Bergues had
kissed her as proxy for Charles, took place
at Greenwich.

Louis' substitute was attired in " a gown
of cloth-of-gold and purple satin in chequers "
with " a most beautiful collar."

Mary looked even more youthful than her
years in " a petticoat of ash coloured satin "
with " an overdress of purple satin and
cloth-of-gold in chequers " to match the
Duke's.   Katharine of Aragon walked beside
her.

After the wedding there was a Court ball,
and then, to make the deed quite irrevocable,
Mary was placed on a state couch around
which specially honoured guests were permitted to stand and the Duke de Longueville
took his place beside her ; one of his gorgeous red boots had been removed and the
whispering courtiers watched while he deli-
cately touched her foot with his. . . .

And now it was Mary's turn to appoint a substitute to represent her at the proxy marriage in France and the honour fell to the Earl of Worcester, who journeyed across the Channel, and, " in the name of the very redoubtable Lady Mary," solemnly accepted Louis " for her husband and spouse," undertaking " to obey him during her natural life."

The fourteen-year-old Prince of Castile was wroth when he heard that he had lost his English bride and bearded his Council only to be lectured on the rights of his elders. " The King of France was the first King in Christendom and it therefore lay with him to take as his queen any woman he chose . . . whereupon the prince used very strong language."

By now Louis had become genuinely eager to receive his youthful bride. He had seen her portrait and been told that she was " beautiful and of a good-figure, being well-grown." Her deportment, too, " was perfect " and she had " no melancholy."

" She has been well brought up," wrote one much impressed Frenchman, " and if one wants to please her one has only to talk of Monseigneur. In goodness, beauty and age there is not her like in Christendom."

Mary's letters signed " by the hand of

your humble companion," heightened his
interest, for she assured Louis that what she
most desired was to hear of his health and
prosperity.

" The King, my brother," added Mary,
" uses great diligence to speed my passage
across the sea, which I hope, by the pleasure
of God, will be brief."

Louis sent commands that Mary be dispatched " right speedilie " and amused himself by overhauling his jewels, deciding to
give these to his bride " not all at once,
but on divers occasions so that he should
have, at different times, kisses and thanks
for them."

Mary rode to Dover accompanied by the
King and Queen, the Archbishops of
Canterbury and York and all the Court, with
" hundreds of knights, barons gentlemen and
esquires " many of whom brought their
wives and daughters. It was a splendid
progress and rarely before had there been
seen so many " gowns of woven gold,"
sparkling jewels and " palfreys in state
trappings."

The parting was long drawn out for a gale
made it impossible to go on board ship
for several days, but at length the seas
moderated and the weeping Princess tore

herself from the caressing arms of Katharine of Aragon and received her brother's
last kiss.

Even as he blessed her on giving her over
" to God, the fortune of the sea and the
governance of the King of France her
husband," Mary reminded Henry of the
promise she had wrested from him. Her
next marriage must be one " as me liketh
for to do " !

The convoy sailed, encountered rough
weather and was separated, but the vessel
having Mary on board made the French
coast and was driven ashore near Boulogne
where gallant Sir Christopher Garneys
struggled to land with her in his arms " not
without jeopardy " ; both were wet and
dishevelled.

A day or so's rest was permitted, and then
Mary passed on to Abbeville travelling by
palfrey and litter and escorted by 2,000
English horsemen and a cavalcade of French
and English nobles, each endeavouring to
outvie the other in the splendour of their
attire.

Mary, a-glitter with jewels and robed in
cloth of silver, looked " more like an angel
than a human being," according to François
de Valois, Louis' son-in-law and heir-presumptive by virtue of his marriage.

The King met her a mile out from Abbeville and "kissed her as kindly as if he were twenty-five" though she was so encased in "goldsmith's work" that she could not dismount as etiquette demanded.

The marriage was arranged for the 9th of October as this was the festival of St. Denys and was as splendid an affair as could be devised, "being solemnised with all honour and joy and royaltie."

Mary looked "right goodlie to behold" with her fair hair flowing loose beneath her coronet, her robes of gold furred with ermine and the élite of the French Court around her decked in brocades and jewels, while "the pomp of the English was as grand as words can express."

There followed a state banquet—"where the English Lords and Ladies were honourably entertained according to the dignity of their persons and to the contentment of all of them that had no dregs of malice or mislike settled in their hartes"—and a ceremonial blessing of the marriage bed.

On the morrow, though Louis gave her a wedding gift of magnificent jewels, Mary sent a frantic wail to her own country, for all her English attendants were dismissed, "except three maids of honour of small

account . . . even my moder Guildford,"
and nothing she could say or do would turn
the King from his purpose.

" Ye would little have thought I should
have been thus entreated ! " wrote Mary
indignantly.

Moved by her passionate grief and realising something of the difficulties of the
position Wolsey made an effort to persuade Louis to let Lady Guildford retain
her old position, but Louis would have none
of her.

" My wife and I be in good and perfect
love," he answered, " and if my wife need
counsel, or to be ruled, I am able to do it."
As for Lady Guildford, " rather than have
such a woman about my wife I had liefer
be without one ! "

His shower of jewels flowed fast ; now a
flawless ruby, now a string of diamonds and
then a rope of pearls.

Suffolk, who had been one of the official
witnesses at the marriage, wrote to Henry :

" There was never a queen in France that
had demeaned herself more honourably and
wiselier, and so say all the noblemen. . . . "
As for the King, " there was never a man that
set his mind more upon a woman than he
does on her, because she demeans herself
so winningly towards him."

Henry VIII was "vastly pleased" and wrote at once to Louis expressing his satisfaction at his sister's behaviour.

"We have heard how she conducts herself towards you in all humility and reverence . . . and our will and pleasure is, that in so acting, she persevere from good to better if she wish and desire our fraternal benevolence. . . . Thus indeed we gave her our advice and counsel before her departure from us."

The journey towards St. Denys was delayed by reason of Louis suffering a bad attack of gout, but at length the slow progress began and the coronation took place on November 5. Mary Tudor was Queen of France.

Suffolk was present and watched infatuated François de Valois as he stood behind Mary's chair of state holding poised the crown which was so weighty that the young Queen's childish head could not support the burden.

Next came the state entry into Paris amid tremendous enthusiasm. Mary in "white cloth-of-gold with a coronall all of great pearls on her head and her neck and breast full of jewels," was carried under a canopy and escorted by a band of Scottish archers commanded by the Duke of Albany, Regent of Scotland, over which country Mary's sister's son was infant King. Three thousand priests and the City Guard came out to meet her, the latter in " coats of goldsmiths work."

". . . and on Sunday," wrote the Duke of Suffolk after describing Mary's royal progress, " by the Grace of God the jousts shall begin."

They began and there were " brave doings " indeed, for " at every course many dead were carried off without notice taken."

The King and Queen had their places on " a goodlie stage," Mary sitting " so that all might gaze upon her and wonder at her beauty, but the King was feeble and lay on his couch for weakness."

The tournament lasted three days. On the first, Suffolk " hurt a French cavalier so that he was like to die," and overthrew a man-at-arms " both horse and man." Dorset, England's second champion, also distinguished himself, " nearly demolishing " an opponent.

Party feeling ran high, " for still the Frenchemen would not praise the English for their prowess." So, towards the end, or so one story runs, " thinking to have the Duke of Suffolk rebuked, the tallest and

strongest man in all France was introduced
quite secretly, for he was a German and of
low degree " !

A terrific combat ensued, " the German
strake stronglie and hardilie at the Duke
and the judges suffered more strokes to be
foughten than was appointed, but when they
saw the German reele and stagger they let
fall the raile between them. . . ." However, after " taking the air " the com-
batants fell to again and continued till the
Duke, by pure strength, " took his assailant
about the necke and pomelled him so about
the heade that the bloude issued out of his
nose and then they were parted " ! The
German was " spirited away lest he should
be known," and " thus the enterprise
finished to the laud of all parties and the
Englishmen received much honour and no
spot of rebuke, yet they were privile set upon
and in manie jeopardies. They had ever
on their apparrell red crosses to be knowne
for the love of their countrie."

The gallants returned to England bearing
letters from both Mary and Louis.

" How lovingly the King, my husband,
dealeth with me, the Lord Chamberlain with
the others of your ambassadors can inform
your grace," wrote Mary.

As for Louis' epistle, its tenor was : " I

know not how I can sufficiently praise and
express my delight in her " (Mary). And so
having written he died within the week
(New Year's Day, 1515). Mary had been
Queen of France for three months. There
were some who shook their heads and whispered that Louis would still be alive if he
had not married a heedless young wife who
inveigled him into gaieties unsuited to his
years, and had changed the hour of his
dinner !

Farsighted Wolsey, conscious of the difficulties that would beset Mary should she be
left a widow, had written warning letters
urging the need for caution, particularly in
regard to the making of promises.

Mary was indignant that he and the King
" should hold me in such childhood " as to
require such advice, but a fortnight later
she wrote urging that Henry should have
her fetched " right speedilie," for " I am
grieved with suits by no means consistent
with mine honour and so diseased with
the tooth-ache that I know not what for
to do ! "

So the Duke of Suffolk, accompanied by
" a goodlie band of gentlemen all in black,"
was bidden to return to France with all haste
carrying " a receipt " which he was em-
powered to give in exchange for Mary when

she, and her dower, should be handed over
to him as the King's representative.

There had been some dispute as to whether
the Duke of Suffolk should be honoured
with the commission, but his enemies with-
drew their opposition when he took an oath
not to abuse his trust " or show any partiality towards the Frenche Quene."

Mary's spirits soared when a way of
escape seemed to be opening before her : " An
if it were to-morrow I would be ready ! "
she cried blithely when told to prepare.

Untoward delay followed and day by day
rumour multiplied the number of possible
husbands for the newly widowed Queen.
Now the name of Charles of Castile her erstwhile fiancé was whispered, now his grandfather Maximilian, or should it be one of
the Dukes of Savoy, Lorraine or Bavaria, or
else the Prince of Portugal ?

To make matters worse some English
friars gained access to Mary and from these
she gleaned that there was a plot afoot ; she
would not be safe even on an English ship,
for its captain might well have orders to
land her on a foreign shore and see her
made an unwilling bride once more. As for
the Duke of Suffolk she was bidden place
little faith in him since he had " traffickings
with the devil."

But to these last innuendoes Mary refused to listen. Instead, she defied the friars and summoned Suffolk.

" Never saw I woman so weep ! " said the troubled Duke, detailing the story of the interview at a later date.

Mary's letters to Henry grew desperate :

" To the King, my brother, to be delivered in haste," she wrote. " Sire, I beseech your grace that you will keep all the promises that you promised me when I took my leave of you by the water-side. . . . Sire, your grace knoweth well that I did marry for your pleasure at this time and now I trust that you will suffer me to marry as me liketh for to do. . . . If not, I promise your grace that you will hear I have gone where neither man nor woman shall have joy of me—which I think your grace would be very sorry of, and all your realm ! . . . An your grace be good lord to us both I will not care for all the world else and beseech your grace to be good lord and brother to me as you have been aforetime for in you is all the trust I have in the world, after God. . . .

" God send your grace long life and your heart's desire ! "

But Henry was demanding back not only his sister, but her dowry to the last farthing and likewise all the jewels with which she had been decked, even though these were the crown jewels of France.

Had he not been put to " great cost " in preparing her for her marriages, first the abortive affair with Charles of Castile, and then with Louis of France ?

Henry was having a difficult time, for his sister Margaret, Queen of Scots, was also writing badgering letters bidding him " make haste to Scotland with his armies by land and sea." Instead, Henry bade Margaret come to England for refuge, bringing her children with her,[1] and turned again to Mary's affairs.

But François's admiration of his young stepmother-in-law, who was so infinitely more attractive than the wife statecraft had obliged him to marry, had driven Mary to appeal to his chivalry and confess " the good mind I have towards my Lord of Suffolk."

The step was wise and presently the Duke was writing to England telling of his predicament ; of how King François had drawn him aside with talk of " a bruit " that he, the Duke, had come to marry with his master's sister. In desperation he had boldly denied the truth of any such " bruit," only to have the ground cut from under his feet by the

[1] See *Their Majesties of Scotland*, by E. Thornton Cook (Murray).

French King's quiet statement that " the Queen had broken her mind to him on the subject."

" I was abashed," wrote Suffolk, " and the King saw it." But the chivalry which had been awakened in him by Mary's appeal was still strong, so, smiling, he offered the Englishman his hand and told him that, " by the faith of a King," he would advance his cause " with as good a will as I would for my own self ! "

Suffolk's nerve was shaken. He expressed thanks but added that he would be " undone " should the matter reach Henry's ears.

So the interview ended, but it was followed by one yet more startling according to Suffolk's mind, for Mary, alarmed at the snares set for her feet and the ever increasing list of those named as possible husbands, issued an ultimatum.

The Duke must marry her now, at once, or lose her for ever and she would believe that he had been sent merely " to 'tice her home " in order that she might be betrayed into another state marriage !

The wilful Queen had her way and a strictly private ceremony was hastily arranged, François being one of the little group of ten present.

But the ten could not keep the secret and

the story of that night's doings leaked out
highly embellished. The news travelled to
England where a Council was called at which
Suffolk's enemies urged that if indeed he
had done this infamous thing he must be
beheaded forthwith.

Letter after letter was raced across the
Channel. François wrote ; Queen Claudia
wrote at her consort's behest ; and Mary
once again took up her pen " humbly and
heartily " beseeching her brother's consent
to her marriage with the Duke of Suffolk,
" for all the love he bore her."   Once again
she reminded him of his promises " as before
rehearsed," and bravely accepted the burden
of guilt.

" I did put it to my Lord of Suffolk's
choice whether he would accomplish the
marriage in four days or else he should never
have me, whereby I know full well I constrained him to break such promises as he
had made your grace." She begged that
Henry would write " some comfortable
words " to " my Lord of Suffolk."

Suffolk was in sore need of " comfortable
words," for he realised with appalling clear-
ness the jeopardy into which he had slid. He
availed himself of the shelter that was
offered, and his letters, like Mary's, told the
story of her sudden assault on the citadel of

his heart, emphasised her weepings and her terror, and the dramatic demand for an immediate marriage; for the hero of a hundred tournaments his stand was hardly heroic.

" . . . and I saw me in that case that I thought it better rather to put me at your highness's mercy than to lose all, and so I granted thereto—and she and I were married."

On Wolsey was flung the burden of an answer :

" With sorrowful heart I write unto you. . . . No man can be more sorry than I that you have so done," he wrote frankly. . . . " Cursed be the blind affection and counsel that hath brought you here unto ! " But at least he went on to outline a plan by which it was conceivable that pardon might be won.

There must come further humble letters from the culprits and from their aiders and abettors the King and Queen of France, after which it might be well if Mary and Suffolk should undertake to pay over to Henry the larger part of Mary's dower, her " plate of gold, her jewels, her dot. . . . This is the way that you shall make your peace, as well as by other true ways. . . . Now I have told you mine opinion hardily

follow the same and trust not too much
to your own wit," he wrote admonishingly,
and ended with a warning that the Duke
was " in as great a danger as ever man was ! "

The two knew it, and if money could buy
safety they were willing to make any
sacrifice. The only question was as to
whether sufficient could be wrested from
François to satisfy Henry, for he had protested that if Mary kept France's heirlooms
she must accept too the burden of the late
King's debts. Now, seeing her predicament,
he waived the stipulation and presently
Mary found herself with all her " gold and
jewels, her apparrall and household stuff "
handed over " by indenture to the Duke of
Suffolk."

With a light heart she drafted a letter
on the lines advised by Wolsey and sub-
mitted it to him for correction.

" Dearest Brother, I doubt not that you
have in your remembrance that whereas for
the good of peace you moved me to marry
with my late lord King Louis (whose soul
God pardon !) for the furtherance of your
causes, I was content to conform myself to
your notions (although he was very old and
sickly) . . . so that, if I should have the
fortune to survive the late King, I might,
with your good-will, marry myself at my

liberty without your displeasure. . . ."
Turning to later events Mary explained how,
" on account of the virtues she had per-
ceived in my Lord of Suffolk," she had
determined to marry him, " and this without
any request or labour of my lord's," added
Mary with the frankness of a modern maid.
" To be plain your grace, I have so bound
myself unto him that for no cause earthly
will I vary or change. . . . So now my good
and most kind brother I beseech your grace
to take the matter in good part."

Realising the large sums Henry had spent
upon her " marryings " and in arranging her
return to England, " to my great delight and
signal comfort," Mary hoped he would accept
her jewels and plate together with such a
sum of her yearly dower " as shall stand with
your good-will and pleasure."   As an earnest
of her intentions Mary sent across her magnificent bridal diamond.

She added an appeal that Henry would
no longer be " miscontent with my Lord of
Suffolk " and said that he and she would
remain at Calais " until such time as I shall
have an answer from you of your good and
loving mind . . . without which, I will . . .
no further enter your realm."

To Suffolk's relief and Mary's joy such a
reply reached them that they dared to

" take shippe " and cross to England where Mary, with her " winnings in France " amounting to nearly £100,000 worth of jewels, found herself received " right heartilie."

A deed was prepared by which Mary undertook to pay Henry a thousand pounds a year for twenty-four years in addition to handing over her " winnings," and after this, since Henry preferred to ignore the private marriage in Paris and questioned the validity of a second which had been celebrated in Calais on the ground that it had been performed " in Lent and without the publication of banns," a third ceremony was arranged at Greenwich where the whole Court attended.

Hardly had this been achieved when Margaret Queen of Scotland made her appearance, having fled from her latest husband,[1] and in honour of his two sisters Henry ordained some " solemn days of justes," when he faced all comers with the Duke of Suffolk by his side as in the brave days of old, " which was a sight to see. Every man did well but the King did best . . . and so at night all ceased and came to supper."

[1] See *Their Majesties of Scotland*, by E. Thornton Cook (Murray).

These excitements over, the Duke took his bride and "departed into his countrie" for a while, for "having spent liberallie on his journies when he went as ambassador, and also in the solemnyation of his marriage, and his Housekeeping since he was married, also having borrowed good sums from the King which he hoped would have been forgiven him but the Cardinal would not have it so," Suffolk was financially embarrassed.

The two were allowed little peace, for Henry was capricious and would now summon them to Court and then as suddenly banish them. There were yet more difficult occasions when the King's favour rested on the one and not on the other.

Children were born, and since the birth of the eldest daughter Frances coincided with a period of royal favour Katharine of Aragon and the baby Princess Mary were permitted to accept the office of godmother ; Anne Boleyn was sent to represent them.

The gods must have laughed ironically as they watched the group around the font. The maid-of-honour who was to cause the divorce of the Queen she served and the disinheritance of that Queen's daughter before she herself went to the scaffold—the baby she sponsored, destined to be the mother of Lady Jane Grey who for nine

dramatic days usurped the crown[1] before
she followed Anne Boleyn to her tragic death.

When an embassy came from France to
negotiate a marriage between the Dauphin
and Princess Mary, child of Katharine of
Aragon, " the Frenche Quene," as even
Suffolk called her, was summoned to assist
at the reception of the ambassadors and play
her part in Court theatricals.

But their stay was short, for Henry was
in financial straits and remembering that
Suffolk was still in his debt he began to press
for payment ; Duke and Duchess stole away
to economise. Then Mary's health failed
and Suffolk was constrained to write to
Wolsey on her behalf :

" The Frenche Quene is ill," he explained,
" and has taken a phantasy that she must
come to London for the remedy. . . . She
weeps all day."

Afraid that she would do herself an injury
Suffolk was anxious to use " all diligence in
bringing her to town." Might she have a
lodging in the Court, " be it but one chamber
so that it shall not be said she be out of
favour ? My lord, all her trust and mine is
in you," he ended humbly.

Either Wolsey's good offices or Mary's

[1] See *Her Majesty : The Romance of the Queens of England*,
by E. Thornton Cook.

pathetic appeal to Henry " that the sight of him would be the greatest possible comfort to her," had their effect, for the two were permitted to come to Court where " the expense of the Frenche Quene's dyet " was carefully charged against her !

Mary recovered quickly and was fair enough to dazzle Charles V, once that Prince of Castile to whom she had been betrothed in babyhood, the hero of the first of her many marriage ceremonies, when he came to pledge himself to the infant Princess Mary.

There were other visits to Court, where the atmosphere had changed. The King's " secret matter " was being discussed and Katharine was refusing a divorce, fighting a losing battle for her daughter's sake.

The Duke of Suffolk but not the " Frenche Quene " went with Henry to France when that King took Anne Boleyn with him instead of Katharine of Aragon.

The turn of events terrified Mary, Duchess of Suffolk. If Katharine of Aragon could be set aside and the Lady Mary declared illegitimate, what of her own daughters Frances and Eleanor, for the Duke's matrimonial adventures had been varied. In his hot youth he had fallen in love with one Ann Brown ; having contracted himself to her his erring fancy had strayed to another charmer, Margaret Mortimer; but a marriage with her proving unsatisfactory he secured a church decree of invalidity and married Ann. At one period he had been contracted to one of his wards.

Clear-sighted Mary had obtained a " Bull " at the first hint of trouble and doubly to safeguard her daughters had it attested, so preventing Margaret Mortimer, now known as " alias Brandon," from laying claim to the Duke, but she watched the progress of Anne Boleyn with a sinking heart.

Then : " This year (1533) on Midsummer eaven died the Frenche Quene, sister to the Kinge and wife to the Duke of Suffolke." They gave her a grand funeral " with a dole provided in four places in the town, having meat and drink come who would, and every poor body 4d."

There was a scene in the Abbey when the daughters of the Duke's repudiated wife appeared and Frances and Eleanor had to withdraw, but Mary Tudor was safely dead.

Two hundred and fifty years later her coffin being opened it was found that the " Frenche Quene's " hair was still vital. Walpole secured a lock; another century passed and the relic was offered for sale in a London auction room.

CHAPTER IV
PRINCESS OF THE REALM
1516–1558

MARY TUDOR

Born (at Greenwich) .	.	February 18, 1516
Crowned . . .	.	August 30, 1553
Married (at Winchester)	.	July 25, 1554
Died	.	November 17, 1558

Descent

Elizabeth of York *m.* Henry VII
|
Henry VIII (and others)
m. Katharine of Aragon (and others)
|
Mary
m. Philip of Spain

CHAPTER IV

PRINCESS OF THE REALM

" Vampyre Calumny shall prey on my remains : My name
shall last to frighten the children of the race I love ! "
Aubrey de Vere.

SIXTEENTH CENTURY

" By the Grace of God sons will follow,"
said Henry VIII when on a Monday morning (February 18, 1516) he learnt that at
last he was the father of a living child.
Public rejoicing was spontaneous, the people
lit bonfires while oxen were roasted whole
and wine flowed in the streets so that all
might feast and drink to the health of the
little Princess.

A silver font was brought from Canterbury to Greenwich for the christening ceremony and Wolsey, Lord Cardinal of York,
the Duchess of Norfolk and the Countess of
Devon were selected for the honour of god-
parentage from among the throng of eager
claimants.

" God give good life and long unto the
right high, right noble and right excellent
Princess Mary, Princess of England and

daughter of our sovereign Lord the King ! "
cried the heralds with a fanfare of trumpets.

Margaret Plantagenet, Countess of Salisbury was appointed Mary's principal guardian with the wife of Sir Thomas Bryan as
" Lady Maistress " to superintend the household. The staff included several nurses at
twenty pounds per annum, a washerwoman
paid at the rate of 66s. 8d. a year and a Chaplain or Clerk of the Closet at the scarcely
princely remuneration of 6d. a day.

The popularity of the baby Princess was
an expensive matter for her harassed guardians, since bearers of gifts had to be re-
compensed and on such occasions as New
Year's Day presents poured in upon Mary
from all sources. At one end of the social
scale was the servant of the King's sister,
Mary Tudor, Queen of France (after whom
this new Princess had been christened)
bringing " a pomader of gold," to whom not
less than 20s. could be offered ; at the other,
" the child of a poor woman " with an offering of apples, who had to be rewarded with
11d.

Before Mary was eighteen months old she
had started on her career of god-mother by
accepting moral responsibility for Frances
Brandon, daughter of " the Frenche Quene."

(Thirty-six years later Frances's child, Lady Jane Grey,[1] was to snatch the crown from Mary.)

Soon after this Mary took on a new importance, for the much desired Dauphin had been born in France and negotiations for a marriage between this infant and England's Princess were begun.

The King of France sent envoys and Mary was carried to the conference that they might see her.

" Priest ! Priest ! " she cried in delight on seeing a visiting friar, sure that she recognised a friend.

The preliminaries being satisfactorily settled, peace was proclaimed between France and England, the terms being read before the high altar at St. Paul's, and in proof of Henry's sincerity he swore that he would never cut his beard until he had visited his " good brother, Francis." Francis took a similar oath, so bringing beards into fashion in France, but Henry broke his word, offering as an excuse the plea that " the queen objected " to hirsute adornment, so making much trouble for the diplomats.

A formal betrothal between " Ladie Marie the King's daughter " and the Dauphin of

[1] See *Her Majesty : The Romance of the Queens of England.*

France was arranged. The baby bride wore
cloth of gold with a velvet cap on her flaxen
curls, and played with the ring the Cardinal
of York placed on her finger while the Bishop
of London delivered a powerful oration in
praise of matrimony.

The betrothal was conditional on the consent of the principals being given when they
reached legal age, when the marriage was to
be " firm and stable or else not, for that
were very wrong."

In the event of the marriage taking place
and the issue of that marriage mounting the
throne of England, France agreed to pay
Henry's heirs " a hundred thousand crowns
a year for ever . . . and for sure payment
of the sums of money to be paid to the King
of England five gentlemen of the realm of
France were sent to England as hostages ;
three were of noble blood, but the other two
were of mean houses." All the hostages
were so young that " ancient gentlemen "
had to accompany them as their governors.

The marriage contract was to be fulfilled
when the Dauphin reached the age of fourteen, Mary and her dower then to be sent
to France. That country was to allow her
an income " as much as any queen of France
had," and Henry, well pleased, agreed to
allow himself to be excommunicated, and

England laid under interdict, if he should fail to keep the contract.

Great preparations were made for a meeting of the Kings in connection with this marriage " betwixt our deerest doughter the Princess and the Dolphin of Fraunce," Francis offering to meet Henry at " Calays." Henry " condescending thereto accordingly, bade Sir Adrian Fortescue with ten tall personages well and conveniently apparralled for the purpose prepare to pass with him beyond the seas," when besides " finishing the marriage " Henry was to " deliver agayn the citie of Turney that he had conquered and since builded a new castle which cost him many a thousand pounds."

Before long news of happenings in England reached Spain, causing some disquiet, for Charles frowned on an alliance between France and England, but being at the moment engaged to a Portuguese Infanta he could do little more than hint at his own willingness to marry Mary if need be. France was pressing for a ratification of the treaty and attempting to dazzle Henry on the Field of the Cloth of Gold, where Henry went accompanied by perturbed English envoys ; for it was well known that search had been made throughout France in order that the fairest ladies in the land might out-

shine the English women on this occasion.
But Mary Tudor, now Duchess of Suffolk
but invariably called " the Frenche Quene,"
had been summoned from retirement and
saved the situation by " outshining all " to
the joy of the English.

Her namesake, Princess Mary, too young
to ride beside her father, remained at Richmond where French envoys and the Lords-
in-Council travelled by barge to visit her
during her parent's absence " and found her
(lauded be Almighty God) right merry and
in prosperous health daily exercising herself in virtuous pastimes and occupations,
whereof we saw some experience before we
departed from her." Mary was "right honourably accompanied by noble personages" too,
these being " as well spiritual as temporalle,
and her house well-furnished with a number
of goodlie gentlemen and tall yeomen in
addition to divers gentelwomen," these too
being " well apparralled."

The four-year-old hostess entertained her
guests " with goodly countenance and proper communications," even playing on " her
virginalls " to them so that they " marvelled
greatly and rejoiced, her tender age considered." After the performance " goodly
chere " was made, the envoys being feasted
on strawberries, wafers and wine, at a cost

of 35s. 1d. according to Mary's household
account-books.

When so excellent a report of Mary
reached France, gifts of " scent and smocks "
were dispatched to her forthwith, and Francis
even consented to Henry's demand that the
Dauphin should be sent to England when
he had celebrated a few more birthdays.

Life flowed on peacefully for a year or so
while Mary's list of god-children lengthened;
but strings were being pulled and presently,
much to the satisfaction of Katharine of
Aragon, her nephew Charles came to England
again and agreed to marry Mary when she
was twelve years old " or forfeit half a
million crowns."

This new betrothal was secret, and it
was agreed that " peace with France was
to be dissembled " until such time as Henry
and Charles were ready to strike.

As the future consort of an Emperor
Mary's household was increased. She now
had six gentlemen to attend her, fee'd at
7½d. a day, 10 varlets at 3d., a stable boy
(three farthings dearer than a varlet), together with three children of the kitchen and
a woodbearer paid at the rate of 1d.

Perhaps the six-year-old Princess forgot
her latest betrothal in the excitement of
the Christmas festivities arranged for her

a few months later when there were " goodlie
and gorgeous mommeries," no less than
three " furious and fell boars " being purchased for the occasion, while a band of
" mommers " were hired and provided with
" a giant hobby-horse, coney skins and tails,
armour and gold-foil bells," all for her
amusement.

Mary was in high favour. Henry even
dispatched a special embassy to ask the
advice of Margaret of Savoy in connection
with his daughter's trousseau, so anxious
was he " that the princesses apparaill for
her persone shall be according to the facion."
Patterns of the selected materials were sent
over and Margaret was " prayed to devise
the makings thereof."

But before long Charles began to have his
doubts as to Henry's intentions ; it was
evident that France was stirring, while
Wolsey was giving diplomatic consideration
to a proposal from James of Scotland. To
clinch matters Charles sent a demand for
the immediate delivery of Mary, in order
that she might be brought up in Spain.
He required her dowry also, so that it
might be spent in invading France.

The request occasioned consternation in
England and commissioners were hastily
appointed in order that they might visit

Spain and assure Charles that all rumours
were false.   There had been no negotiations
with France and as for the King of Scotland
Henry had "refused all," even though
James had offered to "abandon France for
evere" if Mary were given to him as a
bride.

If Charles still showed himself difficult
after hearing this the commissioners were
to try to soften him by pointing out that
"it was not meete that one so tender in age
should be called upon to endure the paines
of the sea," and to be "transported to ayre
that might be dangerous to her person"!
However, there were conditions on which
Henry would risk the sending of his daughter;
Charles might have her if he would hand
over the King of France to Henry to be held
by him as a hostage until Mary came of age
to marry—"although the Frenche King
might be thought an insufficient pledge and
surety for so great a princess"—and if,
having provided Francis as a hostage,
Charles would assist Henry to his "rightful
possession," the French crown.   This
achieved, Henry would himself deliver Mary
—in Paris—after his coronation!

The negotiations were long and cere-
monious.   It is not clear how much of their

master's purpose the envoys unveiled, but
a special ambassador was speeded on his
way to Spain bearing an emerald ring as a
gift from Mary to Charles.   It was a superstitious age and the message with the ring
laid stress on its occult properties ; perhaps
the token would help Mary to a better
knowledge of her fiancé " when God shall
send us grace to be together."

Charles, aged twenty-six, "thankfully"
accepted the ring from his nine-year-old
fiancée and made dutiful inquiries as to her
health and learning, "which," said the ambassador making his report, " we declared
unto him the best we could, showing him
the manifold seeds of virtue that were in
her grace."

But the young monarch was not content
with Henry's promises that Mary should be
formed by her mother " in the manner of
Spain," for he was fast increasing his power.
Perhaps, after all it might be wiser to marry
the Portuguese Infanta rather than this
daughter of Henry VIII.

The King of France was a prisoner in
Charles's hands and bid for Henry's help
by offering himself as a bridegroom for
Mary if she could be " a corner stone in a
new covenant between England and France!"

But Charles, the conquering Emperor,

had another matrimonial project in view
for his prisoner, even though he himself had
decided to jilt Mary Tudor, daughter of
Henry VIII, as he had jilted Mary Tudor,
daughter of Henry VII.

Knowing little, and doubtless caring less
about the various matrimonial possibilities
before her, Mary, " our deerest best beloved
and onelye doughter," had been sent,
" accompanied and established with
honourable, sadd, discreete and expert
counsayle," to reside in the Marches of
Wales with the title of Princess of the
Realm, and authority to hold " Courts of
Justice." The child had three hundred
" sage persons " in her train including the
Countess of Salisbury, and various school-
masters, chaplains and apothecaries.

A year or more before this Katharine of
Aragon had had a paper of " instructions "
drawn up for her use in connection with her
small daughter's education.

" Governed by these," wrote the tutor,
" except all human expectations fail, holy
and good she will be by necessity." Books,
of a type that would " improve her morals,"
were to be chosen for the Princess by " grave
and learned preceptors." Poetry was not
on the list, being considered " pestferous."
Dictionaries were permitted under restric-

tions, for Mary was to be forbidden to learn " naughty words." For lighter reading she might " study such narratives as those concerning Joseph." She was to be " made familiar with the works of Plato, Cicero and Seneca and to memorise a certain amount of Latin and Greek each day." If Katharine decided that it would be beneficial for Mary to have young companions to study with her, all conversation between the children should be conducted in Latin.

Now that Mary was going to Wales these instructions had to be supplemented. Those in attendance on her were bidden to see that she was trained " in virtuous de- meanour," and taught, " at due times," to serve God. French, music and dancing were to be added to her list of accomplish- ments, and her apothecaries were directed to have regard to her " dyet, which it is meete should be pure, well-dressed and served with comfortable, joyous and merrie com- munications."

The Princess should be encouraged, too, " to take the ayer in gardens, sweete and holsome places," while " the cleanleness and well-wearing of her garments, and the apparel both of her chamber and her body " were to have strict attention. All " cor- ruptions, evil ayres and things noysome and displeasaunt," were to be " forboren and eschewed."

Popular songs were sung about this " right joyous and merry " Princess who kept court at Ludlow ; she was described as " wise and sage and beautiful in favour," while authors hastened to dedicate their books to " the second Mary of the world in virtue, grace and goodness."

The Princess was recalled from Wales in consequence of the negotiations for a French marriage, the advantage of this being, in Henry's eyes, that it would bring about a definite break between Charles and Francis ; but though Mary was described as " the pearl of the world," and Wolsey produced a Papal message to the effect that a union between Mary and the King of France would be re- garded as " holy," the matter hung fire.

Charles had a firm grip on Francis and Mary was very young. The most satis- factory agreement that could be reached was that Mary and Francis should marry if he remained a widower until she reached a possible age ; otherwise, the Duke of Orleans would fulfil the contract.

England was not pleased ; it was felt that " the Princess of Wales " was worthy of something better than a second son, but in the innermost circles there were whispers.

It was said that the French ambassadors had questioned Mary's legitimacy.

In blessed innocence Mary danced in the Court ballet, but the star of Anne Boleyn was rising and at Christmas when " XX li " was paid to Mary " to disport herself," a full " CX li " went to " Lady Anne."

A few months later there was talk of " the King's secret matter." But Katharine of Aragon was fighting for her rights, and those of her daughter ; Anne Boleyn grew bolder and the King more ardent, " sore lamenting " that he was still chained to his brother's wife.

When Mary was eleven years old divorce proceedings were begun, but Katharine's letters to her daughter still deal mainly with her studies.

What progress is she making with her Latin ? She must forward her exercises to her mother, after correction, in order that she may see for herself, and in reply Mary sent her a prayer she had translated from Thomas Aquinas :

" O merciful God, grant me to covet with an ardent mind those things which may please thee. . . .

" Good Lord, make my way sure and straight to thee that I fail not between prosperity and adversity, but that in pros-

perous things I may give thee thanks and
in adversity be patient. . . .

" Make me to lift my heart oftentimes to
thee, and when I fail make me to think and
be sorry with a steadfast purpose of amendment. . . .

" My God, make me humble without
feigning, merry without lightness, sad without mistrust, sober without dullness, fearing
without dispair, gentle without double-
ness. . . .

" My Lord, grant me wit to know thee,
diligence to seek thee, wisdom to find thee ! "

The trend of affairs was watched anxiously
by Eustace Chapuys, the Emperor's ambassador, who was under no illusions.

" The moment this cursed Anne sets foot
in stirrup," he wrote to Charles, " she will do
all the harm she can to Queen and princess."
There were those who said that she would
" give Mary too much dinner," or " marry
her to a varlet," when once the girl fell into
her hands. Others whispered that the King
intended to force Mary into a convent to
make the road clear for any children he might
have by Anne.

At last Henry's thin patience snapped and
he rode away from Windsor with Anne,
leaving orders that Katharine and her daughter must leave the Castle for different locali-

ties before he returned. They obeyed and
never met again.

Bitter with the knowledge of her mother's
wrongs Mary was summoned to be present
at the birth of Anne Boleyn's child, and attended Court with the Countess of Salisbury
where they found the air heavy with rumours
and scandal.

The herald who proclaimed Elizabeth's
title announced Mary's fall, and she rode
away with a much diminished escort though
the people cheered her lustily.

Katharine was ill, and Mary, forbidden to
see her mother, wrote anxiously for news :

" I am in the case that the long absence of
the King and you troubleth me," came the
Queen's non-committal reply.

And now a messenger carried a letter to
Mary bidding her lay aside the title of
" Princess " and she, her Spanish pride
ablaze, gained time by decreeing the messenger as " of so little account " that his
message could not be " hearkened to." The
fellow even failed to impress her servants,
" notwithstanding the commands being so
high and weighty," as he reported to those
that sent him when recommitting the matter
unto them, " trusting the Holy Goost have
your Lordships in his most merciful tuition."

Following up her first defiance Mary wrote

to her father explaining how she had been shown a letter in which she was mentioned only as " the Lady Mary the King's daughter," and " marvelled at it," certain that he was not privy to any such communication. She signed herself Henry's " most humble daughter," but added the word " Princess " under her name.

Punishment was swift. Mary was forbidden to come to Court and Henry's wrathful outburst over her " Spanish obstinacy " started a report that he intended to send the defiant girl to her death.

Katharine heard the rumour and wrote a panic-stricken letter bidding Mary " obey the King in everything except only that you will not offend God and lose your own soul." She should " speak few words, avoid disputation and meddle nothing, until this troublesome time be past." Above all she must learn " to offer herself to God with a merry heart " !

Mary might have found it easier to go to the scaffold than to obey the next command that reached her, for she was summoned to Hatfield to attend on Elizabeth.

The Duke of Norfolk was the bearer of the order and Mary told him that the proposals he brought were " most unfitting."

He answered that he had not come to dispute but to see the King's commands obeyed, and the greatest concession Mary could wrest from him was the delay of half an hour. In this brief time she copied out a protest that had been drawn up for her by Chapuys, in the hope that it would safeguard her rights should this be but the first step towards " persuading her by deceit " to renounce these, marry against her will, or take the veil.

While the scared Princess wrote, Lady Salisbury did her best to persuade the Duke of Norfolk to allow her to continue to serve her young charge " at her own cost," if need be, " and with a good and honourable train of servants." But the Countess found herself summarily dismissed, and when Mary rode away she was allowed to take with her only two attendants.

With these, the obdurate Duke delivered her at Hatfield still refusing to use the title of " Princess " in connection with Elizabeth, although, recognising that the younger child was her father's daughter as well as Anne's, Mary compromised by offering to call her " sister."

The Act of Succession was passed, disinheriting Mary since her mother's marriage was " unlawful " and settling the crown upon Anne's children, but Katharine of

Aragon refused to accept the position of Princess-Dowager and clung to her title of Queen even though Henry threatened to punish her by withdrawing his " princely estimation, goodness, zeale and affection," from Mary.

The Princess was being " straightlie kept," because when she appeared in public the people cheered her " as if she were God Almightie himself, just descended from Heaven, and for this some were sent to the Tower, but she contrived to write a formal letter of protest against the decree that had defamed her mother and herself. Threats left her undaunted.

Charles V, advised by Chapuys that Henry if he did not behead Mary would force her to marry " one of base blood," wrote concerning the " mistreatie of his aunt and her daughter," so arousing Henry's indignation.

He replied that rumours of his " mistreatie " of Katharine were quite unfounded, while as for " our dowghter the Lady Mary whom we do entertayne as we thinke most expedient, and also as to us seems pertynent, we think it not mete that any persone should prescrybe unto us how we should order our own dowghter, we being her naturall father."

But though Mary had been " most ungoodlie, obstinate and inobedientwise," having " wilfullie resisted, sett at naught and contempted his will," he might legitimise her, might even use her as " our dowghter " if only she would " cease resisting " against his laws !

Anne, too, was trying her hand at taming the resolute spirit of her difficult step-daughter, and when visiting Elizabeth at Hatfield told Mary that, in exchange for recognition of her position, she would use her influence with the King on Mary's behalf.

" I know of no other Queen in this realm than my lady mother," answered Mary, and Anne retired vanquished.

But the battle had been long and the burden was too heavy to be borne by girlish shoulders. Mary fell seriously ill when a statute was framed requiring " all the craftis in London to sweare to be true to Queen Anne and utterlie to forsake the Ladie Mary but a bastard "; all the priests and curates throughout England were required to "sweare " to the same effect.

Chapuys believed that some slow poison was being administered and warned Lady Brian (Anne Boleyn's aunt), who had charge of both Princesses, that she would be the first suspect could such a plot be proved. The good lady knew her own danger and was

" wont to towring her hands and weep,"
whenever Mary was ill. She must have
had a harassing time, for there are a pathetic
number of payments made " for the letting
of her grace's blood," during the period
Mary remained in her care.

Katharine was as alarmed as Chapuys and
appealed to Henry urging that Mary should
be sent to her, for " the comfort and cheer-
fulness she would have with me would be half
her cure," but the King remained firm in his
determination to keep mother and daughter
apart.

Seeing no other certainty of safety for the
unfortunate Princess, Charles and Chapuys
made tentative plans for rescuing her and sent
Spanish ships up the Thames, but Mary
was closely guarded and the scheme fell
through.

A fresh turn to events was given by
Francis, who, in the hope of making a
definite breach between Henry and Charles,
suggested that the old treaty should be
revived and the betrothal between Mary and
the Dauphin carried through.

Anne Boleyn saw an insult to herself in the
proposition, so goaded Henry sent a reply
to the effect that if the Dauphin wanted a
wife he might marry " the true princess,"
Elizabeth ; when the envoys arrived ex-

pecting to be received by Mary they found
her little half-sister awaiting them in due
state, while Mary was a prisoner in her rooms.

It was clear to Henry VIII that there
would be scant peace while Katharine, " the
obstinate Spaniard," and her daughter stood
in his path, so vowing that he would make
such an example of his recalcitrant child
that no other in his realm should dare dis-
obey him he sent a message to Parliament
bidding the members find some way to
" release " him from his former wife.

Katharine's death saved the situation.
The Commons breathed more freely while the
Court rejoiced with Henry's eye upon it.

" Now I am Queen indeed ! " cried Anne
Boleyn and a fanfare of trumpets preceded
Elizabeth on her royal progress to Mass.

Mary felt that the death that had hovered
over her during girlhood was very near ;
even Chapuys was powerless to help her,
and all she could do was to " prepare to
offer herself to God with a merry heart,"
as bidden by her mother.

Then came a flicker of hope. Jane Seymour caught the King's wandering eye and
she had been Mary's friend.

Anne fell. Elizabeth's baby triumph was
over and her mother went to the block.

Without loss of time Mary wrote to

Thomas, Lord Cromwell. Intercession, she
knew, would have been useless " during that
woman's lifetime," but now, could he not
help her towards a reconciliation with her
father ?

The statesman seemed benign, so, in
obedience to his advice the Princess drafted
a letter to the King and forwarded it to
Cromwell for correction. In this she undertook to " submit to the King next to God
Almighty," and begged only that she would
not be forced to go against her conscience.
The limiting phrase was considered
" offensive " and although Mary protested
that she had used it " most naturally," it
had to be deleted. This acquiescence
induced Cromwell to venture further, and
he sent a " book of articles " for Mary's
signature.

The dismayed Princess found that she
was required to confess that she had
" obstinately and inobediently offended the
King," but that now, realising her own
ill doing, she was prepared " to submit
herself to the laws of the realm, acknowledge
Henry as the supreme head of the church,"
and even worse, " admit that the marriage
between his majesty and the late princess-
dowager had been unlawful, both by God's
law and man's."

The pill was too bitter. Mary refused to sign and all believed that her life hung on a hair.

Chapuys came hastening. If life could only be bought at the price of dissimulation, she must dissemble, for it was her duty to live.

A council sat in secret session and Chapuys continued his urgings. Almighty God would judge her by intentions, not by acts, and when she had signed, absolution could be sought from Rome.

Accustomed to accept spiritual dictation Mary wavered and when the " confession " was again placed before her, together with an ultimatum from Cromwell, she yielded, signed—and then sent an imploring appeal for a dispensation.

At Court the atmosphere underwent a sudden change, for Henry came a-riding to visit the pardoned Princess, bringing Jane Seymour with him to receive bridal congratulation. When " the comfortable tidings " of Henry's third marriage had reached his elder daughter, Mary had ventured a letter in which she referred to the new consort as her " natural mother, the Queen."

But Henry had high hopes of a son, so for the time being both Princesses were left

at Hunsdon. Elizabeth was now officially
considered as " base-born," but Mary ignored
the fact when she wrote concerning her and
showed courage if not tact :

" My sister Elizabeth is in good health
(thanks to our Lord) and such a child as I
doubt not but your highness shall have
cause to rejoice of in time coming."

The months passed swiftly and in the new
tranquillity Mary busied herself with music
and needlework, and studied " philosophy
and mathematics," while Henry, impatiently
awaiting the birth of his child, toyed with
the idea of marrying his elder daughter
now to the brother of the King of Portugal,
now to the son of the King of France. He
might even give her an ample dowry if she
would kiss his feet " for the best father ever
woman had."

Once again authors dedicated their books
to " this noble King's daughter," and wrote
that the " virtue of her looks excels the
precious stones." Once more she found
herself in demand as a god-mother ; in one
year Mary stood sponsor to fifteen children
of all classes and in her carefully kept
accounts are records of the sums she spent,
in gifts for her god-children of gentle birth,
and in paying apprenticeship fees for others.

Various entries show the Princess's girlish

interests. She purchases hempseed for her birds, and a " kennell " for her greyhounds. " Strawberries and creme " cost her quite a considerable amount, and " paid for money lost at cards," appears regularly ; Mary was an unlucky player !

And now the birth of Jane's child was imminent and Mary was summoned to Hampton Court having signed her renunciation of rights of succession in favour of the unborn baby. Hand in hand with Elizabeth, her first supplanter, she walked in the Prince's torchlight baptismal procession.

A few days later Mary was called upon to kneel " lamentable-wise " beside Jane's coffin ; she ordered 1,200 masses for the repose of the dead Queen's soul.

For a short period the Princess now took the position of first lady in the land, and in the intervals of Court duties spent her time embroidering tiny garments for Jane's son, and trying in vain to make her allowance of £40 a quarter meet the increased demands made upon it ; but her losses at cards were heavy and the god-children numbered a hundred. However, she was sufficiently in favour for Henry to pay without comment a dentist's bill of 45s. " for the drawing of the Lady Mary's teeth."

But the state of the country was disturbed, there were murmurings and risings to extinguish which the ringleaders had to be " put to death in such number at one time as never yet was heard of."

To make matters worse, Reginald Pole (son of the Countess of Salisbury) whom it was rumoured Mary loved, was urging that Papal action should be taken against Henry. He was beyond reach but the furious monarch struck where he could, and the Cardinal's mother and elder brother were accused of " treason against the King's majestie," and sent to the Tower.

When sentence of death was passed on the Countess her son wrote that she was " condemned to eternal life."

Mary had been sent to Havering with Edward and Elizabeth, but in any case she would have been powerless. The few she could help were of lesser rank, and for these she did her best even to the writing of characters for those seeking new posts :

" Although this man is not my servant," she wrote of one, " yet, because he was my mother's, and is an honest man, as I think, I do love him well and would do him good."

Although Mary was of considerably less importance since the birth of her half-brother Edward, occasional, tentative pro-

posals for her hand were still received.
Among these was one from the Duke of
Cleves who, incidentally, made a bad break
in etiquette by expressing a wish to see
Mary's portrait before a conclusive stage in
the proceedings should be reached. Cromwell wrote the reprimand all felt was due,
pointing out that no precedent could be
quoted for "a King's daughter of High
Degree" having her picture sent abroad for
approval.

But word had been brought to Henry that
the Duke had a sister who had been "most
straitly" trained, and he saw in her the
ideal wife he had been seeking since Jane
Seymour's death.

The King's marriage with Anne of Cleves
made Mary's union with the Duke impossible, but when Philip of Bavaria came to
England to be present at the King's wedding
he offered himself as a substitute, and Mary,
though "professing a desire to continue a
maid all her life," was brought to accept
him. Duke Philip kissed her, gave her a
diamond cross and went off to arrange for
the ratification of the marriage treaty.

But Henry had not liked Anne of Cleves
on their first meeting, and having married
her, much against his will, he "liked her
less."

Two hundred clergy helped him to freedom and Anne became " sister " instead of wife ; in the disturbed waters of state this broke the slender tie between Mary and Philip ; the diamond cross had to be returned.

Yet another Christmas passed, but financially at least it was an easier one for Mary, since at her request Cromwell had been " a suitor to her father," who thereupon gave his daughter a hundred pounds. Mary was able to buy five yards of yellow satin at 7s. 6d. a yard to make " a kirtle " for Elizabeth and give her young sister " pocket money to play withal."

Edward had " a coat of crimson satin embrowered w' gold," for the work on which " the Lady Marys Grace paid liijs " and as many pence. She also apprenticed several more of her hundred god-children, gave money to various poor people who had brought her homely offerings, and tipped Elizabeth's nurses.

The interlude of tranquillity was brief, for Henry, having married unwilling Katharine Howard,[1] was busy uprooting heresy from the land.

" . . . This yeare the 8th daie of Maie

[1] See *Her Majesty : The Romance of the Queens of England,* by E. Thornton Cook.

Mr Richard Farmer, grocer, a man of grand
substance, was arraigned in the King's
Bench at Westminster of certain seditious
words spoken by him against the King's
majestie, whereof he was condemned to perpetual prison and all his lands and goods
made forfeit to the King and his wife and
children thrust out of doors, which was
great pitie. . . . He was a gentle person and
well behaved in the cittie and had married
his children to great marriages."

But he had denied the King's supremacy
as head of the Church.

Worse was to follow. Mary's old schoolmaster was burnt at Smithfield with her
mother's chaplain, and soon afterwards the
axe which had long hung suspended over
the neck of her first guardian fell. " . . . On
Fridaie and the morrow of Ascension Daie,
my Ladie of Poole, Countess of Salisburie
. . . was put to death for treason against
the King's majestie " ; her seventy years
did not save her.

Before Mary had recovered from another
breakdown Queen Katharine Howard had
been executed " for many shocking de-
meanours though some do suppose her to
be innocent," as runs the record.

Henry was a widower once more and
Edward was said to be delicate. So yet

again Francis mooted the subject of marriage and offered the Duke of Orleans as a bridegroom if Henry would grant Mary a million crowns as a dowry, but Henry thought less than a quarter of this sum should be sufficient, for, after all, Mary was " a King's daughter, with, as yet, but one boy between her and inheritance, and he pointed out that the King of Scots, who had married Mary's aunt, had asked a mere hundred thousand. The matter fell through as the Duke vowed that he would rather accept Mary " in her kirtle " than with " such a meane jointure."

As usual Henry's own matrimonial affairs moved to quick fruition, and presently the daughters of Katharine of Aragon and Anne Boleyn were summoned from their refuge at Havering Bower with the son of Jane Seymour to witness their father's sixth marriage.

Katharine Parr might well have been Mary's sister so far as age went, but she was blessed with the gift of tact and contrived to inaugurate a reign of peace. She saw to it that Elizabeth and Edward pursued a systematic course of study, encouraged Mary's reading, fetched her to Court in her own litter when she was ill, and, when she was well, gave her such pleasures that ten-

year-old Edward feared for his sister's soul
and wrote most earnestly to his third stepmother. He wrote to Mary, too, but not
often, although, as he explained, he loved
her very much " in the same way as I love
my best dresses but do not wear them
often."

By Katharine's influence both Mary and
Elizabeth were restored to such a degree of
favour that they were named as inheritors
of the crown in the event of Edward's death
without issue, always supposing a lack of
heirs " by our entirely beloved wife Katharine
that is now, or of any lawful wife that
we shall marry," as Henry arranged in his
will.

No wonder that the Emperor Charles
was suggested once more as a consort for
Mary and, to safeguard eventualities, the
Prince of Spain for Elizabeth !

But Henry was busy warring in Scotland
and in France, and before he was free to
come to grips with the marrying of his
daughters " it pleased the Almighty God to
call to his mercy that famous Prince
Henry VIII . . . whereupon Parliament,
the executors of the King and others of the
nobility assembled themselves together, and
first by sound of trumpet in the Palace of
Westminster, and so through London,

caused his son and heire Prince Edward to
be proclaimed King."

Mary's letter of congratulation was one of
the first to reach the new sovereign and he
wrote to her immediately, promising " so
far as in me lies I will be to you a dearest
brother."

A wave of enthusiasm for the young King
swept the country, for he was " the beauti-
fullest creature that liveth under the sun,
yet passes he not the age of ten years," as
one of his admirers explained, " and his
goodness increaseth with his greatness."

The Princesses were relegated to the background while the nation concerned itself
with getting the King married. Should his
bride be the young Queen of Scots ? Pro-
tector Somerset demanded her at the point
of the sword,[1] but her mother had different
plans and " knit her in marriage to the
Dauphin."

Others suggested a French Princess, but
though France was willing to provide a bride
for Edward, and deliver her, " at her father's
charges, three months after she was twelve
years old, sufficiently jewelled and well
stuffed," no agreement could be reached as to
a dowry. A small party urged the suitability
of Lady Jane Grey, granddaughter of Henry's

[1] See *Their Majesties of Scotland,* by E. Thornton Cook.

favourite sister, who had played with Edward
in his nursery.

Even on Sundays there was no respite
from the subject, for Latimer thundered from
his pulpit that " the Kynge must chuse
unto hym a godly wife . . . whereby all
godlynes shall increase and righteousness
be maintained. . . . A proud wanton one,
full only of treasure and worldly pomp,"
must be avoided.

But the first marriage in Court circles
after the death of Henry VIII was that of
his widow Katharine Parr.

Before her father had been five months
in his grave Mary received a letter from
Sir Thomas Seymour (who had she known it
had already made suit to Elizabeth [1]) urging
her to use her influence to persuade the
Queen to marry him quickly.

Mary answered that this was " strange
news," and explained that she could hardly be
" a meddler in the matter," " seeing whose
wife her grace was of late," but she begged
Sir Thomas not to take her refusal to aid
him as unkind, for, " wooing matters set
apart, (wherein being maid I am nothing
cunning)," she would be " glad to do him
pleasure."

The affair had given Mary a shock,

[1] See *Royal Elizabeths*, by E. Thornton Cook (Murray).

however, and she thought it hardly proper
for Elizabeth to continue under her stepmother's charge, so suggested that the
younger girl should come to her.

" Princess and very dear sister," wrote
Elizabeth in tactful refusal of the invitation,
" the best course we can take is that of
dissimulation. . . . Silence," if it did them
" no honour, . . . will not draw down upon
us such disasters as our lamentations might
produce." So she elected to stay.[1]

Visits to Court can hardly have been
pleasant experiences, for when the young
King spoke he had to be answered on
bended knee, and even Mary, his elder sister
and heir-presumptive to the throne, might
not sit on a chair at his table but only on a
bench, and this had to be sufficiently far
distant to ensure that she did not come
under even the fringe of his royal canopy.

Both Princesses were glad to withdraw
themselves, and Mary went to live quietly
in Essex, coming to Court only when summoned and finding increasing comfort in
her religion. She wrote for herself " A
Meditation touching Adversity " : " All
adversity should be to us as spurs with the
which we, being dull horses, or rather asses,
are forced not to remain long in this tran-

[1] See *Royal Elizabeths.*

sitory way. . . . Wherefore, Lord, if thou
do add a weight of adversity, add thereunto
strength that we shall not be overcome
with that burden, and give us grace never to
will but as thou will. . . . So be it. Amen."

When the Act of Uniformity was passed
inflicting penalties upon those hearing mass
in the old form she ignored it, and protested
indignantly when notice reached her that
she must use the English service in place
of the Latin mass.

Had not six men and women been burnt
in Coventry in her father's day for the crime
of having taught their children the Lord's
Prayer and Commandments in the English
tongue? and now she was bidden to commit
a worse sin.

" I see men whom my father made from
nothing take usurped power upon them,"
she said bitterly. . . . " He put them in
trust . . . they have broken his will and
made laws contrary to the law of God, of
the Church . . . contrary to the law of all
Christendom ! . . . If you have forgotten
my father, God has not suffered me to forget
him, and I will keep his laws as he left them
until my brother comes to years of discretion."

The long struggle had begun, for such
behaviour could not be ignored.

Mary was told that her house was a centre of sedition. Her chaplain was bidden, " see to it that she hath not her mass but the communion and other divine services as set forth by his majesty " ; and Edward, " marvelling at her refusal of obedience," thought it must be caused by " a certain grudge of conscience for want of good information to remedy it," and promised his sister " prelates to instruct her ! "

Mary answered that her " soul was God's " and her faith she " would not change."

Edward replied that he " constrained not her faith . . . but willed her as a subject to obey the law." The example she was now setting " might breed too much inconvenience."

Mary remained obdurate and the Council summoned the recalcitrant Princess to town :

" The XV daie of March (1551) the Ladie Marie rode through London into St Johns Clerkenwell her place, with 50 knights and gentlemen in velvet coates and chaines of gold afore her, and after her three score gentlemen and ladies everyone with a black rosarie . . . and when she arrived at Westminster the Kynges grace mett and salutyd her."

The superstitious crowds who had thronged the streets to see Mary pass whispered that

they had seen soldier forms in the clouds
and that these had drifted down to earth
before becoming invisible ; they were full
of foreboding.

" My sister came to see me," wrote
Edward in his journal, " and was called
by the Council into another room where it
was declared to her how long I had suffered
her masses . . . in hope of her reconciliation, and now, having no hope . . . except
I saw some sort of amendment I could not
leave it."

The Council bade this difficult Princess
" instruct herself by reading the grounds of
Protestant belief," but Mary answered that
she had " never read any Protestant books
and never intended to do so."

The fight was on with a vengeance.
Fifteen years before, when fearing for her
life, Mary had turned to her mother's country
for help.   Now, molested in her faith and
in terror for her soul's welfare, she again
applied to Spain, and once more Spanish
ships were sent to the rescue of an English
Princess.

Suspicion was aroused.   Mary's every
movement was watched and the harassed
Council, after long sitting, turned to the
bishops for advice.   These deliberated all

night and in the morning delivered the
desperate decision that while " to give
license was sin, yet if all haste possible be
observed, to suffer and wink at it for a time
might be borne in cases that were not without
hope of reformation . . . whereat the Kyng
wept " !

But Mary would " make no haste," with
her Masses, and held her services with open
doors.

One of her chaplains was arrested and
Mary appealed to Edward on his behalf.
A deputation brought her the answer in a
letter which she kissed " because the King
had signed it " ; as for its contents, they
were merely " the doings of his councillors."
Impervious as ever to the arguments they
advanced she reiterated her determination
not to use any other service than that
ordained by her father, and persisted that
laws made since his death did not affect
her. His present majesty, " although a
good sweet Kyng," was " too young to be
the judge of such things."

The unhappy deputation returned only
to be ordered to interview the obstinate
Princess again, " and do better." One
member had courage to rebel, the others
ventured once more and were routed. Mary
was ready to obey the King's laws, " my

conscience saved," indeed she would suffer death for his good—but she would go to the block sooner than forgo her Mass.

The position was tense, for the Emperor Charles was threatening to break off diplomatic relations on Mary's behalf; Edward was showing signs of delicacy as the result of a combined attack of small-pox and measles; and Mary was heir-apparent.

But Northumberland was beside the puzzled young King dropping deft hints as to the danger to the country while the question of the succession to the crown was left indefinite, till at last Edward, " when visited by a longe and werie sickness," drew up his pathetic " devise."

In this he avowed himself

" much troubled in mind in that the Ladie Marye and the Ladie Elizabeth being illegitimate and not lawfully begotten—for as much as the marriage betweene our said late father and the Ladie Katharine, mother to the said Ladie Marye, was clearly and lawfully undone . . . and likewise the marriage had betweene our said late father and the Ladie Anne, mother to the said Ladie Elizabeth, was also clearly and lawfully undone . . ."

it was plain that both these " Ladies "

were "disabled to make claime or challenge the said imperiall croune."

Accordingly, Edward named as his successor Lady Jane Grey, by virtue of her descent from his father's sister Mary Tudor. It was in her favour that she had just been married to Northumberland's son, so could bring no foreign prince into the country as a husband.

Edward had drawn up his "devise" none too soon. . . .

"On Saturday being the 8 day of Juli (1553) the Lord Mayor was sent for to the Court at Grenewich by a letter, and to bring with him 6 or 8 Aldermen, 6 Merchaunt Staplers and 6 Adventurers, which he did the same day in the afternoone, and when they were before the Council there was declared secretly the death of the Kinges Majestie, which dyed the 6 day of Juli being Thursday; and also how he had, by his letters patents, ordayned for the succession of the imperiall croune."

But the secret of the King's death had leaked out. It was whispered that "his majestie had died of consumption as the physicians say, of poyson as everybody says."

Matters moved fast. Two days after the Lord Mayor had had the dire news broken to him, Mary wrote to the Council:

" My lords, we greet you well and have received sure advertisement that our deceased brother, the King, son of our late sovereign lord, is departed to God's mercy."
. . . She went on to demand that she should be proclaimed Queen forthwith, and to express astonishment that this had not already been done.

The reply was that Mary was illegitimate and must prepare to submit herself to her " lawful sovereign." Cecil was among the signatories.

So Lady Jane Grey,[1] and not Mary Tudor, was carried in state to the Tower.

" The X day of July . . . by Vj of the cloke began the proclamasyn of Qwen Jane with lj herold and a trumpet blohyng declaring that the Ladie Marye was unlawfully begotte . . . and so went thrugh Chepe to Fleet strette . . . and there was a yung man named Gilbert the Potter taken that time for speaking certain words of the Ladie Marye that she had the right tytle. . . ." As a consequence he was " put in the pillory in the Chepe, and had his ears nailed thereto and then cut off. . . ."

But Mary acted. " On the 11 day . . . came tydinges to the Counsell that the Ladie

[1] See *Her Majesty: The Romance of the Queens of England.*

Marie had proclaimed herself as Quene and heire to the crowne. . . ."

So the Duke of Northumberland " with other lords and knights . . . departed from London towards Norfolke " to suppress the rebellion, " and with him he tooke those who had taken the Ladie Maryes parte."

But Northumberland left a disturbed city behind him, and Norwich, bolder than London, openly declared for Mary, " since King Edward VI has departed this world to God's mercy." Yarmouth was another loyal stronghold, its citizens decided " to holde and kepe the toune for Quene Marye," and sent messengers to signify its " faythfullness and allegeance, which the said Quene took in very good part and promised to requite the tounes dutifulle kyndness."

Not to be outdone, Colchester followed the example set by Norwich and Yarmouth ; indeed this city sent Mary a supply of provisions including " thre tun of beere," sending with the gift a bill for " expenses of delivery " !

By the 19th of July Jane's brief reign was over. . . . " The Lord Mayor when near St Pawles Crosse met certain councillors who spoke to him secretly and bade him summon the sheriffs and gather at Baynards Castle within the hour."

The tryst was kept and the Mayor found
himself bidden to ride with the Councillors

" to the Chepe to proclam a new quene
which was the Ladie Maryes grace, daughter
of Henry VIII . . . which was so joyful
news that all those who heard wept, and
before the Council had ridden on the hill to
St Pawles Churchyard there was such an
assembly that the Lords could scarce pass
by. . . . And when the proclamasyn was read
by Mr Garter-Kinge-of-Armes in his riche
coate, with a trumpeter being ready, there
was such a shoute of people with casting up
of cappes and crying God Sauve Quene
Marye that the tytle of the proclamasyn
was not heard the people were so joyful man
woman and childe . . . it seemed as if all
had escaped from this eveil world and
alighted in Heaven. . . .
    " Benches and tables were set out for ban-
quets, with wyne and beere for alles, and
bells ringing in every parish church in London, and every street full of bonfyres . . .
and on this day was a fellow set in the pillory
for speaking against good Quene Marye. . . ."

One wonders if " Gilbert the Potter," to
whom Mary, in recognition of his loyalty,
made a gift of lands in Norfolk " to be held
by knightly service," had a fellow-feeling
for this sufferer.
Owing to the confusion caused by the

uncertainty as to whether Jane or Mary
was the rightful successor to Edward, the
matter of his burial seems to have been over-
looked, and now, her crown secure, Mary's
thoughts were all for her brother, and to
widespread dismay she gave orders for a
Requiem and Dirge, and Mass for the repose
of his soul. Nor would she listen to those
who suggested that the matter should be
left to Parliament till the Spaniard, Renard,
shook her resolve by pointing out that the
Catholic service was intended for the faithful sons of the Church, and Edward had
lived and died in heresy.

Mary cried out that she could not have her
brother buried " like a dog," but Renard,
following up his first thrust, insisted that a
heretic should have a heretic's funeral at
Westminster, while if she wished it, Mary and
her Court could pray for Edward's soul at
the Tower. This was done but Elizabeth
held aloof and refused to attend either service.

Evidences of religious unrest were soon
apparent though for the moment held in
check by dramatic happenings : fresh risings
against Mary ; a tumult at St. Paul's by
reason of the preaching of a learned Catholic
father ; Mary's proclamation forbidding her
subjects to " revile one another or dispute."

The trial and condemnation of Northumberland, the Queen's suspension of his sentence
for a few days " for the things that concerned
his soul " ; his death to which " so many
came on horseback and afoot that it was a
sight to see " ; and the preparations for the
coronation of this first Queen Regnant.

Mary came riding from the Tower to
Westminster " all marvellously adorned with
mantle of silver and head-dress of gold."

" Her majesty is thirty-eight years of age [1]
and of matchless beauty," wrote a Spanish
scribe, penning his report of the proceedings.
An Italian was less enthusiastic and ended
his description with a brief sentence—" Her
majesty is well enough." A third writer
(one hopes his public was not large) mentioned that Mary was " of low stature with
a red and white complexion " and very thin.
" Her eyes are light coloured and large, her
hair reddish, . . . her nose rather low and
wide. Were not her age on the decline she
might be called handsome rather than the
contrary. . . ."

With Elizabeth in her arrogant youth
riding behind her beside her father's one
surviving wife, Mary reached the Abbey,
where the coronation ceremony had to be
performed by the Bishop of Winchester since

[1] She was thirty-seven.

both the Archbishops were prisoners in the
Tower. . . .

" And thus the Queen's Majesty between
X and XI of the clock was conducted by
two noblemen to the throne . . . where-
from, after her Grace had reposed a little,
she was lead to the four corners of the dais
when the Bishop presented her to the people
as the rightful and undoubted inheritrix
to the crown and royal dignitaries of the
realm. . . ."

" Yea, yea ! God save Queen Mary ! "
came the response.

She lay before the altar while " certain
oraisons " were said over her, was spurred,
girt with the sword of knighthood, received
the kingly sceptre and had the coronation
ring set upon her finger. They gave her
" the great orb of gold and crowned her
with the three crowns, one for England, one
for France and one for Ireland, setting them
one after another on her head . . . and
between the settings the trumpets did
blow. . . ."

Then came the homage, first the bishops,
each taking a vow " to be faithful and true
and to bear faith and truth unto you our
sovereign lady and queen " ; then the
dukes " and the rest of the nobility," each

taking an oath " to live and die with you
against all manner of folk, so help me God
and All Hallows. . . . And so unto Westminster Hall for dinner where the Lord Mayor
and twelve citizens kept the high cupboard
of plate as butlers."

In the middle of the banquet a horseman
in bright armour rode in and cast down his
gauntlet " which then, as none dared to
take it up while he rode round the hall, he
hailed her as true and rightful queen."
Mary thanked her champion, " and gave him
the gold cup from which she had drank
filled with wine."

Though the Queen had had to borrow
£20,000 to meet the expenses of her coronation there was no stint.

" I know for a fact," says a contemporary
writer, " that more than 100,000 ducats
were disbursed at this coronation." Yet,
" it is not the cost," he adds, " which should
be weighed, as much as the due and timely
performance of the ceremonies. These, in
this case, were ordered with such prudence
and wisdom . . . that this magnanimous
queen has given ample employment for the
authors who may desire to write concerning
them. . . ."

The coronation over, Mary's marriage
became the question of the hour and soon

it was seen that Spain's star was in the
ascendant. The seething element of discontent broke loose and another rising
against the Queen sent Lady Jane Grey to
the block, "while 50 of the most eminent
rebels hung on 20 gibbets in different parts
of the city." But preparations for the
marriage went on.

Philip was coming. Mary shut her eyes
to the fact that he came in obedience to his
father's commands, and not as an eager
bridegroom.

The bitter years were forgotten. She was
Queen and wore the crown, not this arrogant
Elizabeth daughter of Anne Boleyn who
proudly refused to admit herself in any
way less legitimate than Mary herself, and
boasted that of the two she was more like
their father.

Philip was coming; the greatest match
in Europe. But the ambassadors arriving
to ratify the marriage were pelted in the
streets, "so hateful was the sight," and when
they rode through the city, people seeing
them pass, "nothing rejoysing helde downe
their heddes sorrowfully."

In her eagerness that all should go
smoothly, Mary wrote personally to the
Mayor of Salisbury warning him that, as

many would repair there needing wine, he
should appoint " four or more of the most
honest of those citizens who hath been used
to provide and sell this commoditie," they
to see that a sufficient quantity was made
and sold at a reasonable price.

He came, this Philip " by the grace of
God King of England, France, Naples,
Jerusalem and Ireland," arriving " with a
navy of VII score sailes, and landed at
Southampton in Hampshire . . . and on
Friday the XX day of July at III of the
clocke at afternoone, the Lords of the
Council and diverse other noblemen most
lovyingly welcomed him, and my lord the
erl of Arendell put a very riche garter about
his left legge, and there he recreat himselfe
after the sea. . . ."

Mary met him " after he had supped at
X of the clocke " (as I am credibly informed)
and each of them " smyled merily on the
other to the great comfort and rejoicing
of the beholders."

Then came the marriage :

". . . on Wednesday, being St James'
Day the XXV of July his highness, (at X of
the clocke) and his nobles, went to the
cathedral and remayned there, (the doors
being verie straightlie kepte) until the
Quenes highness came . . . at half-houre to

eleven . . . when they were shieven and
married by the Bishop of Winchester Lord
Chancellor of England, and then, shortlie to
conclude, there was for certain days after
this most noble marriage such triumphing,
banketing, singing, masking and dauncing
as was never seen in Inglande before by the
report of all men. . . . And as for the riche
and sundrie apparelles whiche the nobilitie
of Inglande and Spain used and wared . . .
it was a phantase and loss of paper and ynke
to attempt description. . . ."

After the ceremonies at Winchester came
those of London, where a great procession
was to take place. Among other preparations " the Conduit in Gracious St was newly
painted " and loud outcry arose among the
city fathers when, at the eleventh hour, it
was observed that Henry VIII had been
portrayed " with a Bible in his hand " !

The tactless artist was summoned in haste
and threatened with imprisonment in the
Fleet if he did not rectify his error before
Mary reached the conduit.

He set to work, bidden to give his majesty
" a mere pair of gloves to hold in place of
the Holy Book," and inadvertently painted
out some of the King's fingers, but the
Queen failed to notice the mutilation and
the artist escaped punishment.

Mary's popularity was intermittent. There were many who believed there was no safety for her while Elizabeth lived and the religious differences between the two increased the Queen's danger. As Edward had tried to coerce Mary, so Mary now tried to coerce Elizabeth, whose friends made an unsuccessful attempt to organise a plot which, had it succeeded, would have sent Mary to join her husband abroad, and put Elizabeth on the throne.

Persecutions increased, a power stronger than the Queen's ordered heretics to the stake ; neither man nor woman, priest or bishop was safe. Less than two years after Mary's marriage the blow fell on Cranmer, " late Archibishop of Canterburie," who was " degraded of his orders on account of his evil life," and burnt at Oxford. On the same day " Lord Cardinal Poole was made priest at Lambeth " and on the morrow " consecrated Archbishop " ! Mary refurnished Lambeth Palace for him, perhaps finding in the occupation balm for her disappointment in not seeing her friend made Pope, as successor to Paul III. She had used her influence in the matter a year or so before and the honour had come very near. Pole had been actually chosen as Paul's successor, but as it was a midnight

decision Pole turned it aside as " a deed of
darkness," and on the following morning
the conclave appointed Julius III.

It was well that the Queen had at hand a
counsellor in whom she trusted, for Philip's
long absences tried her. She grew older
and more wan till hope gave her a sudden
false illusion of youth.

" The Queen is pregnant ! " so ran the
news. Prisoners were pardoned as a thank-
offering and, " with a joyful heart," Mary
made her preparations even to the drawing
up of " the laste wyll and testament of me,
Marye the Quene."

" I, Marye, by the Grace of God Quene of
England, Spayne, France, both Sicillies,
Jerusalem and Ireland, Defender of the
Faith . . . thinking myself with child . . .
although I be at this moment (thanks unto
Almighty God) otherwise in good health, yet
forseeing the great danger which by God's
ordinances remaine to all women in their
travail of children . . . have thought good
to declare my last will and testament. . . ."

She commended her " soulle to the mercy
of God," and asked that her mother's
remains be fetched and laid beside hers
should she die. Her debts were to be paid,
" and those of my father and brother."

Money was left to various religious orders of whom she asked prayers for herself, Philip and her mother ; and money went too to " poor scholars of Oxford and Cambridge," also to " those soldiers as shall be hurt or maimed in the wars and service of this realm."

Mary's best jewel was to go to Philip " to requite the nobility of his harte towards me."

She begged him to be " a father " in his care of her country.

But Mary learnt to know that her hope of a child was vain. The fires burnt more fiercely at Smithfield, and Calais was lost as the result of Philip's activities against France.

The end came :

" On Tuesdaie mornynge between V and syxe of the Cloke, on XVII Daie of November, in the yere of our Lord 1558, at her manner of St James beyond Charynge Cross," Mary " passed out of the transitory Lyffe of theis Worlde. . . ."

There was a lying-in-state in the black-hung " Prevy Chamber where attended Gentilwomen which did pray about her with lights burning and did wache every night with Dirge and Masse."

Later the Queen's coffin was carried to the Chapel Royal where " after souper " there was a " soleme wache by Lords, Ladys and Gentilwomen also, a herald and purseivante attending, which had their allowance of meate and all things according to the rule of the court . . . and torch bearers too."

The final ceremony took place in the Abbey, when, after the " Buryall of the noble Quene (whose soul God pardon), the noblemen and prelates came forth into the face of the people, and Garter-King-at-Arms did declare the style of the new Quenes Majestie :

" Of the most high, most excellent puissant Princess. . . . God save Quene Elizabeth ! . . . With the wich words all the noblemen held up their head and capps . . . and the Bysshop of Yorke he declared an colasyon . . . and all the trumpets blew a blast, and so the Cheif Mourners, and the lords and knights and the bysshops and the Abbot went into dinner, and all the officers of the Quenes court. . . ."

There was no dole given at the Abbey "for that there should be no report of poor people for the annoyance of the Estates." Instead, alms were dispensed at various churches, " for the saying of the Dirge and Mass for the soulle of this most excellent

and most puissant prince . . . and so ended
the interment of the said Queen Mary." [1]

But there was an aftermath : the Bishop
of Winchester preached too eulogistic a
funeral sermon and received a cautionary
reprimand from Court.

" She was a King's daughter, a King's
sister and a King's wife, she was a Quene,
and by the same token, a King also. . . ."

[1] For the story of Mary as Queen see *Her Majesty :
The Romance of the Queens of England.*

CHAPTER V

" IN HER LIFE SHE WAS
LOVELY AND PLEASANT "

1605–1607

MARY STUART

Born (at Greenwich) . . April 8/9, 1605
Died (at Greenwich) . . September 16/23, 1607

Descent

Mary Queen of Scots *m.* Lord Darnley
|
James VI (of Scotland), I (of England)
m. Anne of Denmark
|
Mary (and others)

CHAPTER V

"IN HER LIFE SHE WAS LOVELY AND PLEASANT"

SEVENTEENTH CENTURY

THREE-QUARTERS of a century had elapsed since the son of pale Jane Seymour was born at the English Court, so for a month previous to the " down-lying of that most excellent princess Queen Anne " (of Denmark) daily prayers were offered up for her safety, and " there was great suit made for offices."

A carnation-coloured velvet-covered cradle fringed with silver was prepared for the eagerly expected infant, together with " carnation velvet mantles " to match, a " head-sheet of cambric embroidered all over," veils and bibs of " fine lawn with others to wear under them all wrought with gold and coloured silks."

The days of penury that had irked Anne when Queen of Scotland were over, so she gave full rein to her love for pretty things and spent three hundred pounds on the baby's layette.

The child was born at midnight (April 8/9, 1605) and the usual exclamations of disappointment at her sex were soon forgotten in the excitement of the official rejoicings. Bells were rung and bonfires lighted, while a royal proclamation described the new arrival as " a most beautiful princess."

A baptismal ceremony, " more splendid than the memory of any one in England could record," was arranged for " the Christninge at Greenwich of the daughter of the mightie King James." The chapel was hung with

" velvet and cloth of gold, all the nobilitie being present. . . . At the tyme when the Royall Infant should be brought to the Chapell the children of that place went out 2 and 2 in their surplesses unto the nurserie doore. Then following them came the Deane of the Chapell, next after the Arch Bishop of Canterburie, both in rich copes of needlework. . . . Then, all returning, came the noble Babe who was carried under a cannapee of cloth of goold . . . the gosypps sat upon 3 several rich stools . . . 4 earls sonnes wayted at the 4 corners of the cannapee. The King with the prince, the earls, bishops and barons, were ranged on one side of the chappell and the great ladies on the other."

A " gentleman-usher " brought word from the King to the " gosypps signifying his pleasure what the name of the child was to be,"

EFFIGY OF PRINCESS MARY, DAUGHTER OF JAMES I AND
ANNE OF DENMARK.

The other tomb is of Mary's baby sister Sophia.   Mary is lying on
her bier, Sophia is in the cradle.

and the Archbishop, with the assistance of two deans, christened her after her grandmother, Mary Queen of Scots.

The "songe of thanksgiving" having been sung, the heralds " put on their coates " and " Garter-King with a loud voyce proclamyne what was his dutie to do. . . ."

Trumpets blew, then " the God Fathers and God Mothers made their offerings," each being fetched from their seats by the Lord Chamberlain; their gifts were carried to the communion table by " the six best noblemen." After this " certain knights and lords barons brought in a bason and ewer and towells and the gosypps washed " when " a great bankquet was brought out of the Lower Chappell " and presented first to the washed " gosypps " and then " to other great personages, the organ playnge aloud all that tyme." Finally the " Child was carried back to the nurserie doore. . . ."

Less than three years later this little Princess Mary was the occasion of another stately ceremony, for " prayers prevailed not for her long life, Divine Providence haveing otherwise determined."

The Court and Lords-of-the-Council were assembled in Henry VII Chapel to listen to a funeral oration preached over her bier by the leading divine of the day.

" . . . The death of the late excellent and
most noble princess (which I will not say
was untimely, though it were early—for she
fell not like fruit that groweth out of season,
but betimes—she was ripened and most fit
to be gathered) may teach our young not to
be confident of life," he began, and went on
to point out that the " receptacle of the body
where the soul lodged was not *domus* but
hospitium (not *home* but a *lodging*) whence
we could be turned out at the pleasure of
Mine Host. . . .

" You have here the body of a princely
infant . . . if the benefit of any privilege
might have exempted and secured her, no
question but that she would have been
rescued from the jaws of death. . . . The
tabernacle of her house was but newly
reared . . . it had a royal and kingly foun-
dation and all the noble ornaments and sup-
portestations that might have upheld it in
strength and beauty. . . . But the house
wherein she lodged was a weak house of
claye. . . .

" She was one of the four corners that so
gorgeously upheld the majesty of the Kingdom. . . . In her life she was lovely and
pleasant and such was the manner of her
death that it bred a kind of admiration in us
who were present to behold it. . . . I goe. . . .
I   goe ! — a   confident   look — Awai   I
goe ! . . ."

The prelate paused, then went on to trust

that the Princess had " now happily arrived with little tossing in a tempestuous sea at the Shore of Blessedness and the Land of Peace."

The congregation was comforted by being reminded that " the royal stock whereon the noble bunch grew doth still flourish," for " many olive branches still stand about the King's table."

Poets of the day wrote of the baby Princess as " a spotless Virgin sweetly singing her Halleluiah to the King of Kings," and beneath her effigy on the tomb beside that of her cradled sister in Innocents' Corner is a chiselled inscription :

" I, Mary, daughter of James, King of Great Britain, France and Ireland, and of Queen Anne, received into Heaven in my early infancy, found joy for myself but left longings to my parents. . . .

" Ye congratulators condole! She lived only two years, five months eighty-eight days. . . ."(?)

CHAPTER VI

"DISCREET AND DEBONAIR"

1631–1660

MARY STUART

Born (at St. James's Palace)   November 4, 1631
Married (at Whitehall)   .   May 2, 1641
Married (in Holland) .   .   November, 1643
Died (in England)   .   .   December 24, 1660

Descent

Mary Queen of Scots *m.* Lord Darnley
|
James I (VI of Scotland)
m. Anne of Denmark
|
Charles I (and others)
m. Henrietta Maria
|
Mary (and others)
m. William Prince of Orange
|
William III

CHAPTER VI

" DISCREET AND DEBONAIR "

SEVENTEENTH CENTURY

" UPON Friday, about 4 of the clock, the Queen was (God be praised) safely delivered of a Princess who was christened the same morning by reason it was weak, some say, . . . but I have heard it was done to save charges and prevent other christening. The name. Marie."

So ran a message concerning the birth of Mary, Princess Royal, daughter of Charles I and Henrietta Maria.[1]

The baby was attractive, having her mother's deep brown eyes and bright colouring. She was born during the brief spell of happiness the Fates allowed Henrietta Maria and passed her early childhood at Hampton Court with her brother Charles, one year her senior, and James and Elizabeth, her juniors.

By the time Marie de Medici came to visit her daughter Henrietta, Charles's difficulties had begun, but he vetoed his mother-in-

[1] See *Her Majesty : The Romance of the Queens of England.*

law's suggestion that he should permit the marriage of his second daughter, Elizabeth,[1] to William, the only son of Frederick Henry of Nassau, Prince of Orange, thinking such a match beneath consideration. At that moment he was contemplating a union between Elizabeth's elder sister Mary, and the son of Philip of Spain.

A few months later affairs in England took a turn for the worse from the monarchical viewpoint, and in his desperate need of an ally Charles was driven to signify his willingness to accept William as a consort for either Elizabeth, or the more important Princess Royal, if the Dutch commissioners considered the younger child too delicate.

An official embassy arrived from the Prince of Orange and Mary won golden opinions for the way she played her part at the reception.

Negotiations went smoothly. The ten-year-old Princess was to be left with her parents for another two years ; then when she went to her husband's country she was to be allowed forty English attendants as selected by her father. The financial clauses offered no difficulties and the gratified envoys went home to report progress, leaving Charles to deal with Parliament and " acquaint "

[1] See *Royal Elizabeths.*

PRINCESS MARY (STUART), PRINCESS ROYAL OF ENGLAND,
DAUGHTER OF CHARLES I AND HENRIETTA MARIA.

Painted about the time of her marriage to Prince William of Orange.
From a picture in the Rijksmuseum, Amsterdam.

the peers " with that alliance and con-
federacy which I intend to make with the
Prince of Orange and the States, which
before this time I thought not requisite to
do, because that point in which I required
your assistance and counsels was not ready
to be treated on."

Having outlined the satisfactory aspects
of the marriage Charles rose in his royal
robes, and recommending " expedition " left
the lords to " free debate."

Presently young William of Orange came
sailing up the river Thames under convoy
by Van Tromp and attended by a " magnificent train of the chiefest nobles of his
own country."

Strafford was being tried in Westminster
Hall, and Mary, child though she was, went
with her parents and, sitting half hidden
behind the curtains of the King's box, must
have realised something of the tragic drama.
Incidentally she caught a bad cold and had
to receive William in bed, the Prince being
admonished by the King that he could re-
pent and decline her if he thought Vandyke
had " flattered Mary overmuch " in the
portrait that had been sent to him.

But fifteen-year-old William had no such
wish ; he had been well drilled and soon his
Dutch tutor was able to write home an ex-

cellent report on the way his pupil was
carrying himself. "He has pronounced his
little speeches with such courage and good-
will that he has won the love of every one
who has heard him"!

The Sunday after Easter was appointed
for the ceremony which was to take place
without the calling of banns, and in as
shortened a form as the dignity of the
Church would permit, in consideration of the
extreme youth of the little bride.

Copies of the Order of Service in both
French and English were delivered to William's tutors with a request that they would
see that the Prince was letter perfect by
the Sunday; Mary, too, underwent her
drilling.

The day came and Prince William walked
to his bridal "in an Utrecht velvet suit and
cloak all embossed with silver" and attended
by ten pages and as many footmen, all in
sky-blue velvet and silver lace.

The bride, a childish figure despite her
"robe of silver tissue," was led into Whitehall Chapel by her two brothers, Charles and
James. Her hair was "knotted up with
silver ribbands" and she wore a coronet of
pearls; a bevy of fair children in white
satin frocks, as near the bride's age as possible, carried Mary's train and officiated as

bridesmaids ; a governess stood close at hand to prompt her charge if need be.

Henrietta Maria was unwilling to take part in a strictly Protestant ceremony, so watched the scene from a box with her younger daughter Elizabeth who had so nearly occupied Mary's place.

By the King's orders all titles were omitted from the service. William and Mary were " this man " and " this woman."

" . . . And the Dean demanded : ' Who giveth this woman to be married to this man ? ' And the King took her by the right hand and gave her to the Bishop who reverently kneeling received her upon his knee, then rose up and gave her to the bride-groom. . . . The bridegroom laid a little ring of gold on the prayer-book. . . ."

" It was a plain gold ring, without any enamel," as William was to explain to his father later.

" Blessed are they that fear the Lord ! " sang the choir, but the ceremony was not yet over for there had to be a communion service despite the fact that " the time was far spent," and after that a sermon.

The King sent a request that the bishop would preach shortly in consideration for the tired child who was the bride, so the

bishop " taking as his text ' The King's
daughter all glorious within ' applied well
to the present business." He did not
long detain the congregation from the
wedding breakfast and " a walk in Hyde
Park " !

At ten o'clock that night Mary was conducted into her mother's room, with great
formality, and lifted into the huge state bed
all draped with blue velvet and adorned with
white plumes, the room being brilliantly
lighted with " flambeaux of white wax."
Then, while the Queen and the great ladies
of the Court stood on one side of the gorgeous
couch and the bride's state governess and
privileged attendants on the other, the King
ushered in William " in robe de nuit and
pantouffles."

Having kissed Charles and Henry, who
attended him, the Prince clambered into
bed beside the Princess " but lying at a re-
spectful distance from her."

He kissed her " several times . . . very
gently, in the presence of all the great lords
and ladies of England, the four ambassadors
of the United Provinces and the other distinguished personages who had attended
him to London."

After a quarter of an hour or so " the King
told him it was time to go," and William

obediently got out of bed again " to receive
the blessing of the King and Queen."

There was a slight contretemps, William
having lost one of his " pantouffles," but
this being found " near the princess " was
replaced on the Prince's foot. He knelt
to receive the royal blessing and was then
allowed to retire to a bed which had been
made up for him in the King's room.

Next day William wrote a detailed description of proceedings to his father Prince
Frederick Henry, describing Mary as " far
more beautiful than her picture. . . . I love
her very much and think she loves me also,"
he ended, and as he wrote yelling mobs were
fighting their way up Whitehall demanding
the execution of Strafford. But the Court
poet sang :

> " No day more joyful ere did Britain see,
> Both King and people in their mirth agree ! "

A little more than a week later Strafford
was executed and almost immediately afterwards William sailed back to his own
country to join his father in camp.

Affairs in Scotland demanded Charles's
attention and Henrietta Maria waited at
Oatlands with her children, eager for his
return. When he came he found himself
greeted with popular enthusiasm.

The Queen had taken Princess Mary and the Duke of York to welcome the King at Theobalds, and the Lord Mayor, City Councillors and sheriffs of London rode to meet them, " joying in his majesty's arrival."

" We present unto you our hearts and affections," said the Lord Mayor speaking for his lesser brethren.   " True that in this we offer your majesty that which is by just right yours before, but upon this new enlivening and expression be pleased to take them as a new gift."   The children were mentioned as " those fruits of your love and our pledge of a prosperous succession," and the oration ended with good wishes to Charles for " a long reign over us in peace, glory and full contentment."

Small wonder that the King, in accepting the greeting, said that he saw now " how all the former tumults and disorders have arisen from the meaner sort of people."   The great body of the nation was evidently loyal and " untouched by the misreports that had been made."   He, for his part, had returned from Scotland with a " hearty affection " for his people, and was " eager to govern them according to the law and to maintain the Protestant religion."

So, preceded by trumpeters, the triumphant procession went on, travelling " from Kings-

land to Shore Ditch by a fair and clean way "
especially prepared for the occasion as the
old route was impassable " on account of its
depths and foulness." And because there had
been " seditious libels " two companies of
city trained bands were held in readiness to
quell disturbances, while " a man was placed
at every corner."

But Mary saw rather the conduits that
ran with claret and heard the " loud and
joyful exclamations " as the royal party
arrived at the Guildhall, where with the
Duke of York she dined in state beside the
King and Queen.

" The banquet was served up in this
manner : From his Majesty's table to the
dresser stood 80 livery men in ranks about
two yards from each other face to face . . .
one rank receiving the King's meat, the
other the princes at the same time. They
never stirred nor removed from their places
but delivered dish after dish to one another
till it came to the sewers who placed it on the
table. All were entertained so plentifully
that not a man was heard to go discontented
away."

Their majesties had to " repose themselves for a while after dinner " before riding
on to Whitehall through cheering crowds
and past more conduits running with wine.

"The whole day seemed to be spent in a kind of emulation (with reverence be it spoken) between their majesties and the city. The citizens blessing and praying for their majesties, and their princely issue, and their majesties returning the same blessing upon the heads of the citizens with innumerable thanks added thereto. . . ."

The next time Princess Mary passed through the streets with her father was when Charles carried his family to the comparative safety of Hampton Court, while the surging mob shouted for "Liberty" and made threatening gestures.

Realising the seriousness of the position Charles decided that help was essential. His natural ally was the Prince of Orange to whose son Mary was betrothed, and it seemed to the desperate King that the only possible plan was for Henrietta Maria to see him and explain the need for prompt assistance. Officially, she could take the Princess to Holland en route to Spa where, also officially, she must go to drink the waters "for the benefit of her health, this being much impaired by reasons of the false rumours that had been set afoot concerning her."

But the Commons were not to be gulled. They went into Committee and decided

that it would be impossible to afford the
Queen " so much as will support her
journey " !   They expressed disapproval too
of the project to deliver Mary to her husband's people while she was still so young,
" for think of the dishonour that may happen
to this nation in this respect.   The princess
is not of years and so the match may break
and she be sent back."

As for the need for Henrietta Maria to drink
Spa water Parliament was frankly sceptical.

A deputation from both Houses waited
upon the King to explain that " having been
informed that the Queen's distemper proceeds from discontent," it was felt that it
would be a reproach to the nation should
she go out of the country in " dissatisfaction
of mind."   Also, there had been discovered
" a greater quantity of Treasure packed up
than the Queen's occasion and honour required," and the carrying of this abroad
would " impoverish the nation."

Charles understood.   He had to make the
matter clear to the foiled and indignant
Queen who sent a message that she was
ready, " at the hazard of her life," to forgo
Spa, since that was the attitude.   She
thanked the members of both Houses " for
their care for her health and happiness—of
which she hoped to see the effects soon."

So much for words. Charles perfected his arrangements so swiftly that the country could make no counter move. Henrietta Maria, with Mary, embarked at Dover and Charles and his elder sons watched them sail. Mary went weeping for Elizabeth and baby Henry, her brother and god-child. She was never to see her father again.

The friendly shore of Holland was reached, where " her Majesty and followers were bravely entertained upon charge of the States which will be continued to them so long as they are in their territories."

Mary and her mother found a warm welcome not only from Prince William and his parents but also from Elizabeth of Bohemia [1] who, with some of her children, had found a refuge at the Hague.

The first festivities over, the Prince returned to camp and Henrietta Maria travelled about the country ostensibly for Mary's sake, actually pawning or selling the jewels she had contrived to carry out of England. [2]

Charles, Prince of Wales, wrote to his little sister who was finding her footing in a strange land :

" My father is very disconsolate and

[1] See *Royal Elizabeths*.

[2] See *Her Majesty : The Romance of the Queens of England*.

troubled, partly for my royal mother's and your absence, and partly for the disturbances of this kingdom."

And Henrietta Maria, in the intervals of selling her jewels and writing passionately affectionate letters to the King, planned another marriage. If the Prince of Wales married a daughter of the Prince of Orange there would be a stronger tie between the countries and perhaps yet more help would be given ! But her manœuvring was seen by the vigilant States, and, as Charles's fortunes sank lower and lower, even Henrietta Maria was forced to realise that Holland did not consider her son an eligible *parti* for a Dutch princess.

" By the treason of his rebellious subjects the King was being hunted from place to place like a partridge upon the mountains." What fate was before the Prince of Wales ?

Having exchanged her diamonds and Charles's buttons for guns and ammunition, Henrietta Maria left her disconsolate little daughter in the care of her parents-in-law and sailed to lend what help she could to the King she loved.

Mary was still a child in years but she grew up fast as she watched for news of her father fighting for his crown, and of her boy fiancé who was actively participating in the war against Spain.

New guardians composed careful rules for her upbringing :

" It will be necessary to determine the hours of the morning at which the princess makes her prayers to God and is instructed in religion, as well as those at which she eats, dresses and performs her other duties. . . ."

Mary must never be allowed to forget that she was Princess Royal of England and should be taught, " even in her games, the value of honour and virtue."

When she appeared in public it must be under the guidance of " some qualified person " upon whom was imposed the double duty of seeing that her charge's actions were always " such as they ought to be," and that those admitted into the presence of the little Princess rendered her the respect and courtesy that were hers by right of birth.

Worse and worse news came from England as Mary grew old enough to take her place as William's wife. Her mother became a refugee in France ; her father was a prisoner, as too was Elizabeth, and her brothers close held by the Parliamentarians.

There were changes in Holland also where William succeeded his father at an unfortunate moment and unwillingly concluded a one-sided treaty with Spain.

But Mary's love was still with England. She saw to it that prayers for her father's safety were offered up daily and urged William to keep Dutch ships hovering off the Isle of Wight in the hope that Charles might effect an escape.

The King came not, but James, the Duke of York, tricked his guards by Elizabeth's contrivance,[1] stole away in girl's clothing and effected a landing in his sister's country.

When Mary heard of her brother's arrival she forgot Dutch decorum in her joy and ran out into the street to meet him.

The boyish escapade stirred kindred spirits in the English navy and presently five English ships put into Brill asking for an English Prince to command them. Unwilling James had to give place to his elder brother who came hastening from France and sailed boldly up the English coast making a " demonstration " if nothing else, before cooler heads persuaded him back to Holland. But it was impossible for the Prince of Wales to remain idle, and presently Charles went to make a personal appeal to the States-General in the hope of stirring them to intervene on behalf of his father.

[1] See *Royal Elizabeths*.

All he could extract was a promise to send a deputation to intercede with Parliament for the captive King, and to Mary, who had caught the contagion of fear from her brother, it seemed long before " the wisest men in Holland " could be selected, though, urged on by William, the phlegmatic Dutch moved more quickly than their wont.

The deputies sailed, were " blown past Gravesend," but made a landing at Greenwich where they learned that the King's trial was nearing its end.

Making all possible haste to London they interviewed Fairfax, persuaded Cromwell to listen to their arguments, and addressed the Lords and Commons, " who gave up their dinner hour for the purpose."

Monday came. The scaffold was going up in Whitehall but still the Dutch commissioners went from one to another begging, at least, for a postponement of the execution.

Tuesday morning found them still working ; they did not desist till the axe fell.

Amazed horror spread over the Seven Provinces when news of the tragedy reached the Hague, where Mary lay ill.

In addition to the shock occasioned by her father's death she had been shaken by a weird prophecy that was being widely circulated. A woman had slipped a paper into the hands of Amelia de Solms-Braunfels, the Princess Dowager and Mary's mother-in-law, in which it was foretold that William would " have a son by a widow and die of small-pox in his twenty-fifth year! " Amelia had been unable to keep the matter secret, and Mary, who had begun to hope for a child, suffered accordingly.

Her consolation was an outburst of popular enthusiasm for the Stuart cause. There was talk of refusing recognition to a Parliament guilty of regicide and of the recall of ambassadors. Feeling ran high during a debate as to whether the United Provinces should offer bold recognition to Charles's son as King of England in defiance of Cromwell, but the deputies of Holland and Zeeland (the two strongest and most difficult of the Seven Provinces) saw danger, and ultimately a compromise was reached. It was decided that in their compassionate address the Prince of Wales should be called Charles II, without mention of country. The titular King was completely dependent upon his brother-in-law ; William even paid for Charles's mourning outfit and the liveries for his servants.

But the English Parliament ignored Dutch wrath and presently sent an agent to negotiate an alliance. Mary considered it a

double insult that the man chosen should be
Dr. Dorislaus, who had been Parliamentary
counsel at Charles's trial.

When almost immediately after his arrival
the doctor was murdered she refused to show
grief until, as a political consequence, William was compelled to ask Charles to leave
Holland.

Mary and her husband escorted him as
far as the Hague and William paid his
brother-in-law's accumulated debts from his
private purse.   Later the two gave eager help
in equipping Charles when he made his first
throw for the crown and landed in Scotland.

The Netherlands themselves were none
too peaceful, for much against William's will
the States-General had decided upon a reduction of the army and now Holland was pressing for the disbandment of another 28,000
men.   To William as Captain-General, planning a war with England on behalf of his
wife's beloved brother and meditating an
attack on Spanish possessions if French
support could be secured, the very idea of a
further reduction seemed preposterous.   His
strenuous objections secured him the promise
of a personal conference with the authorities
in Amsterdam, to which city he went accompanied by a military escort and six deputies,
whereupon the city fathers shut the gates

and swore that they would cut the dykes
and drown the army rather than admit the
Captain-General so accompanied.

A compromise was reached and certain
officials were deposed from office and flung
into prison as a sop to William's pride, but
he still felt that Amsterdam had insulted
him, and his office, and that he was powerless. Returning to the Hague, moodily
enough, he was stricken with a serious illness
and died (November 1650).

The news that William was attacked by
small-pox had been kept from Mary, and
his death appalled her. In an outburst of
impotent grief she escaped from her attendants and flung herself upon her husband's
body, refusing to believe that he could no
longer hear her voice.

The disaster horrified the people, who
turned angrily upon the doctors protesting
that William had died because he had been
" imprudently allowed to change his shirt
thirty times in a week."

But Mary was unconscious of popular
clamour. She lay in state, mourning on a
black-draped bed in a room with black-
draped walls, and a week later, on her own
nineteenth birthday, her son was born—to be
swathed in ermine-trimmed black robes and
laid in a black cradle !

The States-General had purchased a wonderful Paris bed for the occasion of Mary's accouchement, but owing to William's death it was felt that it could not be offered, so it was left on Holland's hands. Much water was to flow down the canals before a use could be found for it.

The prophecy that had foretold the tragic birth of William's son had come true, but in the stars more was written ; he was to succeed to the throne of Charles I of England.

For the moment the baby's position seemed insecure.

The Republic of the Netherlands consisted of seven provinces, Holland, Friesland, Groningen, Utrecht, Guelders, Zeeland and Overyssel. These had revolted against Philip of Spain, who still held the southern portion of the country, and bound themselves to hold together whatsoever befell them. Theoretically, each province appointed a stadtholder (chief magistrate) but actually several of these offices had been entrusted to the successive Princes of Orange whom the Central Government had appointed Captain- and Admiral-General. The office was elective and not hereditary.

Now, although the States-General were

willing to provide the new-born Prince with a pension, there was much dispute as to whether he should be elected to his father's honours of Stadtholder and Captain-General. The baby was to lose many adherents because he was carried to his christening in a state coach with a royal escort; the democratic party had no wish that he should be brought up to consider himself a petty King.

Worse was to follow, for Mary determined to christen her son Charles, after her father and brother, rather than after her husband and the national hero " William the Silent." The people were thankful when the Princess Dowager took up the cudgels and worsted Mary, who bowed unwillingly to the storm she had raised.

Before this untactful attempt had been forgotten a new cause for Dutch disquiet arose. Mary produced an unsigned will and claimed the guardianship of the baby Prince on the strength of it. So once again Amelia rushed into the affray and voiced the feeling of the majority in protesting that nineteen-year-old Mary was unfit for any such responsibility, and might ruin the boy for love of her English brothers; she was still " Princess Royal of England," rather than " Mary of Orange."

In the end a compromise was arranged, and Mary shared the honour of guardianship with her mother-in-law and the Elector of Brandenburgh, who, by virtue of his marriage to Amelia's eldest daughter, held a strong position.

But no persuasion could induce the States-General to confer his father's honours on the little Prince; in the eyes of the many he was more Charles's grandson, than William's heir. A faction headed by John de Witte used every influence to sever the connection between the republic and the House of Nassau. All that Mary could do was to wait till her boy grew older, and meanwhile work towards the restoration of Charles II to the throne of England.

Every tragedy in the land of her birth but heightened her devotion, and she opened eager arms to her young brother Henry, Duke of Gloucester (whom she had last seen as a babe in arms), when, soon after the death of Elizabeth at Carisbrooke Castle, he was " sent out of the realm to lessen the cost of his keeping by the Commonwealth."

Mary welcomed, too, the loyalists who came flocking from England, among them Edward Hyde with his wife and five children; he, having ruined himself for Charles, was glad to accept the Princess's offer of a house rent free at Breda, which being in Spanish territory did not come under the jurisdiction of the States-General.

The number of the refugees disturbed the Dutch and when an embassy arrived from the English Parliamentarians to suggest an alliance and drop deft hints that the Stuart Princess should not be allowed to make the Hague a centre of sedition, a hot debate ensued and the right of asylum was retained by a very narrow margin.

Mary's indignation was intense and she took pleasure in riding daily past the ambassador's lodging, escorted by her brother and a band of Stuart sympathisers, all behaving in as provocative a manner as was possible.

A rumour of Cromwell's death acted as spark to tinder and the loyalists made open demonstrations of jubilation. Bonfires were lighted outside the ambassadorial lodgings and opponents came into conflict. The States-General protested and the Duke of York had to leave the Hague, much to Mary's indignation.

Hardly had the turmoil died down before a fresh cause of trouble arose, for the Princess Royal and Elizabeth of Bohemia had planned a solemn fast in commemoration of the death of Charles and at the eleventh

hour it was forbidden as likely to offend the
English Parliamentarians.

These were dark months for Mary even
though the suggested alliance fell through,
for Worcester had been fought and Charles
Stuart was " missing." When news came
that he had succeeded in reaching Holland,
disguised as a common sailor, his sister stole
to welcome him in secret, not daring to
betray his whereabouts to those around her.
She gave him clothes and money and saw
him off to join her mother, still an exile in
Paris, but Charles left Buckingham behind
him and soon the Court was agog with a new
rumour ; it was said that the Princess Royal
was about to marry her brother's favourite.

" Malice hath been busy with my name,"
wrote Mary to Buckingham, when an anony-
mous letter informed her of the scandal, and
went on to beg him " not to take it amiss "
if she asked him never to see her again.

But the tale had reached Paris and Henrietta Maria was vowing that she would rather
kill her daughter with her own hands than
see her degrade herself by such a marriage.

Public events turned Mary's thoughts
from her personal affairs. A year before,
England, as a reply to a treaty concluded
between the Netherlands and Denmark, had
passed a Navigation Act claiming the supre-

macy of the seas, and now war began
between England and the Dutch.

The sea battle off Beachy Head " was
such a fight as hath never been known,"
according to official report, and there was
widespread dismay when the English had
the best of the battle. As a result a section
of the people began to murmur that this
trouble had come upon them because they
were false to the House of Nassau, and though
volunteers rushed forward and " ships seemed
to build themselves so quickly was it done,"
the star of Orange rose.

It was balm to Mary's spirit, as she went
in state to see a wonderful vessel which would
" go without sails and might well be called
the bane of the English," to watch the children in the streets wearing Orange colours
and hear shrill voices chant :

> " Although our Prince be very small
> Yet he'll be Stadtholder after all ! "

And when Charles sent her small son the
Garter she joyfully bound a blue riband
around young William's leg.

But the English went on " making ready
a great Fleet though in winter men should
be quiet," and peace was discussed in secret
session, for Cromwell's terms were harsh.
Though every deputy was sworn to silence

the truth leaked out ; England demanded
that the little Prince should be excluded
from those offices which had been held by
his father, and required that the Stuart
Princes should be expelled from Holland.

The maritime war dragged on and Holland weakened. The news was greeted with
jubilation in London, where bonfires were
lighted in the streets while the people
gathered around them to sing psalms :

" Behold how good and pleasant it is for
brethren to dwell together in unity ! "

Mary and her son's other guardians worked
in vain to get the Act of Exclusion annulled,
but Cromwell sent a stern warning that this
would mean a renewal of the war and De
Witte went his way unmoved by accusations
of " secret diplomacy." He had no love for
young Prince William whose father had
suspended the axe over his own father's
head.

The lands that could offer Charles a refuge
were becoming circumscribed. France as
well as Holland had put up the bars and
even the most valiant loyalist lost heart,
whispering that nothing could be done till
Cromwell was killed, and giving eager ear
to a rumour· that Mary was planning his
assassination.

No one knew the titular King's exact

whereabouts, but the States-General, un-
easily conscious that in all probability
Charles was where he should not be, decreed
that a " serious letter " should be written to
the Princess Royal on the subject, " admon-
ishing " her " to signify to the said Lords of
the States of Holland, the sincere and very
truth thereof." The " very truth thereof "
was that Charles was living near by on the
proceeds of Mary's pawned jewels.

In bitterness of spirit the Princess shook
the dust of the Netherlands from her feet
for a while and flung herself into the fun of
Frankfort Fair where she went by barge,
travelling incognito with her brothers.

Henrietta Maria was still in Paris and
working for her children. It seemed impossible to advance Charles's fortunes so she
turned her attention to Mary and schemed
to bring her to Paris in the forlorn hope of
marrying her to the King of France.

Eager to taste the gaieties of a great Court
Mary pawned yet more of her jewels and set
off to be met at Mons by an escort of 600
horse, for France remembered that she was
the grand-daughter of a French King. In
her train, entering into the festivities with
zest, went Anne Hyde whose quick tongue
had won for her the heart of the Duke of
York; despite her youth Anne guarded

the secret well and no one guessed the truth.

> " Mild, modest, affable ; beloved and loving,
>   Discreet and debonair . . . "

So the poets had written of Mary, and Henrietta Maria was proud of this daughter she had last seen in childhood. But the projected marriage did not materialise and at last Mary had to hasten homeward by reason of a message that her son was stricken with small-pox. En route she received word that William's illness was measles, not the dread disease from which his father had died, so she turned aside to see her brothers and ventured to Amsterdam on their behalf.

She persuaded a worthy merchant to advance a sum of money to meet the pressing needs of the Stuart Princes on the security of the royal promise that whichever of them reached the throne would see the amount repaid with interest. The terms were stiff, for the Stuart cause was out of favour, partly owing to the activities of an English agent who was writing home jubilant that prayers for Charles were now forbidden at the Hague.

" Indeed I have stirred in this matter to my very utmost," he reported, " for this praying has made the place a very nursery of cavalierism ! "

He was constrained to admit, however, that the prohibition resulted in " great loss to the poor," since those who came to pray had been generous. These had now withdrawn themselves from the church, even removing " their hangings and cushions."

One minister had resigned rather than obey, so perhaps England would make good the financial loss and see that the vacant pulpit was made " a happy door for doing good in this place ? " It could be if " a person of piety, ability, prudence and moderation " be sent. Any other would

" set things afire. . . . I trust that by such a man it shall come to pass that, whereas the vilest of our nation flocked hither pleasing themselves in the notion of praying for the King (as they call him), they shall now be encouraged for goodness."

Mary found life very dull after her visit to Paris and the lagging years seemed endless while she waited for her boy to grow older. She was emancipated now, for on her twenty-fifth birthday she had claimed the full Regency and so had been instrumental in bringing about a serious loss of territory. There had been a dispute over her recognition as Governor of Orange in her son's name. Amelia's nephew, who

had held the post, refusing to withdraw, this
gave the King of France an opportunity
to intervene and take possession. Each of
William's guardians blamed the other, but
Louis could not be dislodged.

Hoping for distraction Mary summoned
her younger brothers to visit her—the
relations between herself and Charles were
strained as the result of a rumour con-
necting Mary's name with that of Lord
Jermyn. They came, and were officially
ordered to leave the country. The Princess
Royal found herself powerless and the Dukes
left her to take service in the Spanish army
and fight against the Cromwellian forces
now attacking the Spanish Netherlands.

Presently a messenger arrived with a
garbled tale of the capture of the Duke of
York, and Mary was in despair till the story
proved false. Then came more news, good
news this time in the eyes of the Stuart
Princess. Cromwell was " seriously ill." At
all costs she must see Charles !

He came in disguise and lodged at a tavern
while they waited for word of Cromwell's
death and a message that England had
remembered her King.

But Richard Cromwell took up his father's
office and Charles went back to his poverty.
Once again Mary travelled to Amsterdam

for his sake but there was little tangible on which money could be raised. The plate had gone long since and Charles's meals were served on pewter.

And now William too passed out of Mary's hands. He was nine years of age, old enough to go to the University of Leyden ; his mother and grandmother escorted him there and the little Prince began to learn how to be a man.

As a child he had been " puny," so strict rules for his upbringing had been drawn up. He had been kept " out of the hands of doctors, as these often ruin their patients with medicines," and he had been " well grounded in psalms in order that he might have such knowledge of them that they would comfort him in adversity."

Now a tutor and page were sought for, the one to be " not gloomy," the other " gentle and useful." The Prince was to be taught to be " affable and prudent and to conduct himself with dignity." Should correction be necessary it was not to be administered " before the world."

William was to study mathematics, " this being the true science of princes," and such knowledge of religious controversy was to be imparted as would enable him to " answer the arguments of the Roman Catholics." He

must fence, ride, play billiards and tennis,
rise early—and might be allowed " a light
breakfast if the doctor judged it necessary "
before he went to his studies.

And now when hope was almost dead there
came a message from England.   The English
people wanted their King.   Charles came
hastening to Breda and Mary sent a formal
notification of her brother's restoration to
the States-General.

Magnificently forgetful of the past, the
deputies drew up an invitation to Charles
begging him to honour the Hague with his
presence, " where he would find such preparations made for his reception as would
testify the joy of their hearts for the blessings
providence was showering upon him."   At
a special session half a million florins were
voted for Charles's entertainment and no
one murmured when Mary summoned her
son from Leyden to head the deputies who
rode to welcome Charles, who came with
fifty English cavaliers behind him and
English gold in his pockets.

Banquets were ordained, thronging crowds
besought the erstwhile outcast to " touch
for the King's evil," and officials scoured
the pawnshops for the scattered crown jewels
which the States were eager to redeem and

present to the restored King. In addition
they gave him the magnificent state bed
upon which young William ought to have
been born. Had it not been a burden on
their hands for ten long years ?

Presently the English ships came sailing,
and Charles, while he waited for a favourable
wind, rechristened them nearer to his taste.
He would not sail in *The Naseby*, so it now
recrossed the sea as *The Royal Charles*.

The three Stuart Princes returned to
England, Charles to his father's throne, the
Dukes of York and Gloucester to " take
their places in the House of Peers, adding
by their presence two stars of the first
magnitude to that sphere which had of late
been wholly overclouded or at best taken
up by meteors and comets."

The Princess Royal and Elizabeth of
Bohemia (Stuart Princesses of different gen-
erations) planned to follow, but Elizabeth's
invitation never came.

By reason of Charles's restoration Mary's
son took on fresh importance. He was now
fifth in succession to the English throne.
Surely, backed by Charles's influence, she
could wrest his father's honours from the
firm grasp of the States ?

But the Dutch would not be rushed, and
though Zeeland and Guelders wavered to

William's side, the deputies felt they had
gone far enough when Holland undertook
to superintend his education and withdraw
opposition to his future appointment.

This step accomplished, Mary sailed for
England to be received with enthusiasm.

" Bright Guardian Angel ! Since you fled from home,
    We lost our virtue and our innocence.
    We lost our peace—we lost your father too,
    And all's imputed to our want of you ! "

As she passed through the streets one told
another of her virtues. Had she not been
" a sanctuary to the afflicted, a chapel to the
religious, a refectory to those in need ? . . ."
Had she not withstood such sufferings as
were sufficient to break the back of a mere
Christian with a courage far surpassing the
weakness of her sex ?

But the happiness of the restored Court
was of short duration. Almost immediately
upon his arrival the Duke of Gloucester
developed small-pox and died. And now
a storm broke out by reason of an announcement that the Duke of York had been
privately married to Anne Hyde in Breda
a year before, and was threatening to leave
the country if Charles would not recognise
Anne as Duchess.

Mary and her mother were equally furious and eager to believe the worst. Anne's father, fearing for the tottering throne of his sovereign, suggested the beheading of his daughter—and as a grand climax another man stepped forward to claim Anne.[1]

Bishops hung over Anne's bed as she writhed in child-birth, adjuring her to proclaim the truth. . . .

And amid all the turmoil and dismay Mary fell ill. Some said that her disorder was caused by the smoke from the city, others pronounced her trouble as measles, and then it was suddenly realised that she had small-pox.

Fashionable remedies availed little, " no bail was found in physic to defer the execution of her death," though the doctors " opened a vein in her foot." She died on Christmas Eve.

The clergy besought the sorrowing people to remember that " a princess, like the sun, doth set to rise," but " her corpse was waited on by an abundance of the nobility whose inward sighs expressed their grief for so grave a loss. All vowed that the zeal and love of the dead Princess for the King

[1] See *Her Majesty : The Romance of the Queens of England.*

deserved to be written on glass and graven
with the point of a diamond. . . ."

But a week later Lord Craven was writing
to Elizabeth of Bohemia that Mary was
" as completely forgotten as though she had
never been."

CHAPTER VII

"A LADIE OF GREAT BEAUTIE AND EMINENT VIRTUE"

1662–1694

MARY II

Born (at St. James's Palace)		April 30, 1662
Married (at Whitehall)	.	November 4, 1677
Crowned . . .	.	April 11, 1689
Died	.	December 28, 1694

Descent

Charles I *m.* Henrietta Maria

James II
m. Anne, daughter of Edward
Hyde

Mary (and others)
m. William Prince of
Orange

Mary II (and others) . . . *m.* . . . William (III)

CHAPTER VII

"A LADIE OF GREAT BEAUTIE AND EMINENT VIRTUE"

SEVENTEENTH CENTURY

THE birth of Mary, daughter of the Duke of York, "At past one of the clock on an April morning," pleased nobody, although she was announced as being a "ladie of great Beautie and eminent Virtue."

Neither the Duke nor the Duchess was popular and such incidents as the birth of a child revived old rumours.

Had it not been whispered that Anne Hyde (the child's mother) was the granddaughter of a pot-girl who had caught the roving eye of a wealthy brewer and bewitched him into marrying her? Therefore this new-born Princess who was in direct succession to the crown, was the great-grand-daughter of a serving wench, even though niece of the reigning sovereign.

There had been plenty of scandal about the Duchess, too. What if there had been a private contract between her, when she was maid-of-honour to Mary of Orange, and

the exiled Stuart Prince—even one, as the
romantic liked to believe, " written in the
Duke's own blood " ?   All knew that such
a deed would not have held good in a court
of law.   And now here was a girl-child
whom nobody wanted, except perhaps the
infatuated Duke.

Mary's nursery was in her grandfather
Lord Clarendon's house at Twickenham but
she was often at St. James's and Hampton
Court.   She can never have lacked playmates, for both brothers and sisters came
in swift succession to share her establishment,
and Lady Francis Villiers, under whose care
the royal children lived, had six daughters
of her own.

At three years of age Mary was a
noticeably graceful child, trained to " dance
ravishingly," to the delight of the Duke of
York who was seen to play with her " like
an ordinary private father," and of the
Duchess, who, " being one of the highest
feeders in the Kingdom, had already become
so plump that it was a pleasure to see her."
She died when Mary was nine years old,
leaving four surviving children, two of
whom followed her within the year.

It was known that before her death the
Duchess had been admitted to the Catholic

PRINCESS MARY (AFTERWARDS QUEEN MARY II) DAUGHTER OF JAMES, DUKE OF YORK, AND ANNE HYDE.

From a picture by Sir Peter Lely.

faith, though Lord Clarendon, living in
exile since his impeachment for treason,
wrote earnestly to both Duke and Duchess
on hearing of his daughter's conversion,
urging that " some antidote should be taken
to expel the Poyson."

A year or so later Mary was to find a new
playmate in her father's second wife, Mary
of Modena, who came, a most unwilling
bride.[1]

The little Princess was now old enough
to take the part of " a chaste young
nymphe " in Court theatricals, and for her
father to dream of marrying her to the
Dauphin and seeing her a Queen of France.

But Charles had other plans for this niece
who was, after her father, heir presumptive
to his crown, and presently the Bishop of
London came to request the Duke's permission to prepare his daughter for confirma-
tion. James gave it in bitterness of spirit
knowing that the King would never tolerate
her admission to the Roman Catholic
Church. Mary was a child of the state and
her destiny lay in the hands of the sovereign.
Charles was planning for her, not the ambi-
tious marriage desired by her father, but

[1] See *Her Majesty : The Romance of the Queens of England.*

one that would bulwark the throne. What
better consort could be found for her than
William of Orange, his sister's son ?

At ten years of age the orphaned Prince
had been left in the hands of his grandmother and John de Witte, Grand Pension-
ary of Holland and the hereditary enemy
of the House of Nassau.

At eighteen, his country devastated by
war, William had outwitted the statesmen
who held him in tutelage and seized the
reins of office.

But the darkest day had not been reached.
England was ranged with France and the
Bishop of Munster against the Netherlands,
since Charles complained among other things
that the Dutch, " with ungrateful insolence,"
refused to recognise England's domination
of the seas and persisted in " supplanting
our trade." Despite this he still felt the
same " tender respect " towards William's
person as formerly, and had bargained that
the young Stadtholder should have those
parts of the Netherlands not required
by himself and France at the end of the
war.

Terms were offered but the Dutch considered them impossible. France required
twenty millions down and the yearly pre-

sentation of a medal. England demanded " the honour of the Flag . . . yea, that the whole Dutch Fleet shall strike and let fall their top sail for any one English ship," also " the full expenses of the war."

Small wonder that the better element in the United Provinces turned to the descendant of their hero " William the Silent," while the mob rent its fury on the fallen statesmen the De Witte brothers, and having murdered them carried their stark, mutilated bodies to the gibbet and hung them head downwards.

At twenty-two William was Stadtholder, Admiral- and Captain-General, having been elected to the offices held by his father.

The Prince reorganised his army and cut the dykes, so calling in, as the French complained, " an enemy as uncivil as the Dutch themselves " to help him, while the troops offered up daily prayers for " the Fatherland fallen into the hands of the enemy."

On sea and land the tide of victory began to turn. William won back thirty of his towns and Lieutenant-Admiral van Tromp wrote of " brave fighting weather, with victory, so far (God be praised) on our side . . . as for the completion we shall, with good resolution and animosity, dispute for it."

Both sides, it seems, had " fought furiously,
but our side more than the others. . . ."
The English were " 60 sail of men-of-warre
strong with between four-and-twenty and
thirty fire ships. . . ." The French had
" thirty men of warre, the least carrying
fifty guns, ten or twelve fire ships, and, with
pleasure boats, máde up a fleet of a hundred
and forty sail."

At the moment of writing " all were at
anker," said the Admiral, " the enemy busy
doubtless as we are, in repairing and putting
things in order."

Further good news was to follow, for in a
subsequent encounter the Dutch lost " only
fire ships (blessed be God). . . . If the wind
had not blown so hard Van Tromp and De
Ruyter would have kept " close to the
enemy, but seeing God pleased otherwise "
they were now engaged in bringing the allied
ships " into good posture."

The report of Prince Rupert who was in
command of the English fleet hardly tallied
with that of Van Tromp. He wrote that
the enemy had " considerable losses which
they will not easily repair," and that De
Ruyter and Van Tromp had " run great
hazard of being burnt by our fire ships if
they had behaved themselves as they ought
to have done."

Evidently the Dutch did not fight " according to plan."

Soon the States were able to hold a national thanksgiving for a " miraculous victory," and Spain seized the Heaven-sent opportunity to attack France.

The far-sighted High and Mighty Lords of Holland now wrote Charles " a very obliging missive " in order to show the English Parliament their willingness " to quench the fire of war for fear it should spread over all Christendom," but the King refused to abate his demands and asked for " twenty tuns of gold."

The Lords Mediators made a bold throw and offered to accept the English Parliament as arbitrator; meanwhile they went on building ships " with vigor and alacrity," and taxed every man " a 20th part of his daily gain."

When Parliament met to hear the King's speech the House was nearly out of hand, and, though Charles explained that he was " far from being in love with warre for warre's sake," but considered that the right way to peace was to have a good fleet for which " cheerful aid was necessary," the Commons went gloomily into committee to consider " the grievances of the Kingdom."

In the previous summer (August 1673) the Dutch fleet had captured " Nieu Amsterdam (New York) and it was still fresh in the mind of Parliament how, a dozen years before, De Ruyter had brought his ships up the Thames to burn three English men-of-war as they lay in the Medway. A valiant enemy, and one which the Commons felt would make a good ally.

The Stadtholder, too, was an asset. He had visited England during a war interlude, hoping to obtain his mother's unpaid dowry, or a refund of sums lent to the Stuarts while they were in exile, and though Charles had found him a " dull dog," statesmen saw William as " a young man of extraordinary parts and good understanding."

Parliament had its way. Peace was concluded and by the Treaty of Westminster (February 1674) England retook possession of New Amsterdam and christened the settlement on Manhattan Island after the Duke of York, to whom it had been given by the King some years previously.

In an attempt to bring about a general amnesty Charles hinted that Mary might be given to William as a wife, but the Stadtholder, whose name was now known throughout Europe, answered that he was in no position to think of matrimony; moreover, he would not marry unless he liked the disposition of the suggested bride ; he was not attracted towards the usual Court beauty.

However, negotiations were continued and so favourable a report on Mary was received that William let the matter go further. So presently, the Duke of York, having dined with his brother in Whitehall, came back to break the news to Mary that she was to be married to her cousin forthwith.

The Princess broke into floods of tears. In fact everybody wept; " the Duke, the Duchess and the Lady Anne would sit and cry two and three hours together," and it was with painfully evident traces of her unwillingness to be a bride that Mary accepted the formal congratulations tended to her.

William arrived, and society pronounced him " the plainest man ever seen and of no fashion at all."   But a fortnight after the Duke had dropped his bombshell into his daughters' schoolroom Mary went to her wedding, which took place " in her bedchamber at 9 o'clock at night."

Public rejoicing was less than had been anticipated, for London was indignant that the bridal gown had been ordered from Paris.

" A memorable week this," wrote Mary's tutor, Dr. Lake, in his diary :

" The Lady Mary and the Prince of Orange wed, a son born to the Duke of York, the Archbishop of Canterbury died and the Lady Anne developed small-pox."

A few days later Dr. Lake went to take leave of Mary, she being about to leave England " the Friday after," and found her still tearful.

He gave her good counsel " and hoped that the things in which he had instructed her would remain with her," adding that he had been with her seven years and "no person who hath lived so long at court but that did make a far greater advantage of his time than I have done—having gotten but a hundred a year." Would Mary, before her departure, commend him to the King, the Duke and the Bishop of London ? He would " endeavour to requite such favours by being very careful of the right principling and instructing of her younger sister, the Lady Anne " !

A final note in the worthy doctor's diary mentioned that " Her Highness gave me thanks for all my kindness and assured me that she would do all she could for me but was able to say no more for weeping."

Alas, those " seven years " had made a less lasting impression on Mary than Dr. Lake had hoped. Within two months of her departure to Holland he learned that his

ex-pupil was " playing cards on Sunday,"
which dismayed him " for such Sabbath-
breaking would doubtless give offence to
the Dutch."

Worse news was to follow. There came
a report that Mary sometimes attended a
church at the Hague " served by an English
non-conformist minister out of England and
maintained by the States to draw people
thither for the increase of their trade."

The Court to which the English Princess
had gone was in sharp contrast to Whitehall
and soon the maids-of-honour were " com-
plaining and wailing horribly," because it
was so dull.

Mary was too young and unformed to
influence it, or William, who found her
companion Elizabeth Villiers more to his
taste than the child he had married for
reasons of diplomacy. So Mary was left
to herself to read, paint, play at hide-and-
seek in the woods and to make occasional
excursions by barge when all were expected
to knit. Her interviews with William frequently ended in a burst of tears, for he was
making every effort to train her into an ideal
wife and the process was not pleasant.

It was a joyful day when, having heard
of Mary's unhappiness, the Duchess of York
brought Anne on a brief visit to her sister.

Gradually Mary settled down into her new life and became accustomed to marriage ; gradually, too, William's lessons took effect. He, old and serious for his years, kept a close watch on English affairs and his protestant conscience was stirred by his father-in-law's ever increasing attraction towards Rome, which became more noticeable after his accession to the throne.

William grew dour, for he saw the trend of popular feeling and realised that Mary might well be offered her father's crown, and he had no mind to be the husband of a Queen. The position was made easier when Bishop Burnet sounded the Princess and was able to report to William that she was horrified at the very idea of accepting any position that would oblige her to take precedence over William. A wife's chief duty, in Mary's eyes, was to obey her husband ; this though she held the bitter knowledge that even yet Elizabeth Villiers took first place.

Mary and Anne had kept in epistolary touch with one another during the years that had separated them, and Anne had christened one of her many short-lived babies after her sister. Now she wrote Court gossip concerning the child that was expected by their stepmother, and how she was sure no one would believe it to be the Queen's infant " unless it proved a girl."

James, too, was writing to his daughter. He was bewildered at the antagonistic position taken up by the Prince of Orange, but assured Mary that despite her husband's actions he believed she was still a " good daughter " to him.

Other letters came from the Queen. Her baby had been born—how was it that the Prince of Wales was not being prayed for in Holland ?

But all Mary's love and loyalty now belonged to William. She accepted the tale that James Francis Edward was a spurious prince, and the King's approach to Rome, with its inevitable consequences, dismayed her.

" To think that my father should be capable of so horrible a crime, and that, humanly speaking, there is no other way of saving the Church and State than that of my husband going to dethrone him by force ! " she wrote.

In England violent debates were taking place in Parliament. The Commons voted the throne vacant, but the Lords, by a small majority, were " non content." After a lengthy battle agreement was reached and both Houses offered the crown to William and Mary.

William sailed nine days after receiving
his letter of invitation, but judged it wise
to leave Mary behind.   At his farewell interview with her he explained that, in the
event of his death, she must remarry immediately.   Her weeping protest was waved
aside ;   personal inclination must not be
considered : on her would fall the duty of
bringing Protestant children into the world.

Seeking for an avenue of escape, Mary
pointed out that although she had been
married to William for many years she had
had no children, and as God had given her
no child of his she would not want one " by
an angel ! "

But William reiterated his commands and
left a weeping wife to declare a fast-day as
he journeyed towards Helvoet Sluys.   All
she could do in this dark hour was to pray.
Mary feared not merely the ordinary dangers
of war for her husband, but the treachery
of those near his person.   Only a month
before, or so she believed, a plot had been
well laid.   It was discovered that the Court
tailor was a papist and that this man and his
boy, " instigated by James," had poisoned
the Prince's new waistcoat, which only a
merciful decree of providence had prevented
his wearing !

William would have reached England

even more quickly than he did, but on his arrival at the port it was found that the fleet had " consumed so much of its provisions that it was necessary to revictual, and three days of good wind were lost while getting in supplies." Then a gale blew up and beat the vessels back to port, some being " so shattered that it was difficult to unload them before they sank." But though " 500 horses perished for lack of air the States were not discouraged," and at length William was enabled to put to sea, taking with him his banner emblazoned " The Protestant Religion and the Liberties of England. Je maintiendray ! "

His arrival came as a fresh blow to James, who was struggling to establish the legitimacy of his baby son and vowing that, with his children turned against him, he would not resist " a foreign army and a poisoned nation." His chief efforts were directed to securing the safety of the Queen and the infant Prince, and he soon followed them into exile.

A messenger was dispatched bearing an order to Mary. She was to come at once and " be cheerful on arrival so that nobody might be discouraged by her looks."

" I did not sleep that night," wrote Mary, " but lay thinking how much I should suffer in leaving a place where I knew how happy I could be ! " The thought of assuming her father's place was a fresh trouble and she prayed that " God would give her a resigned will," then her spirits rose at the thought of seeing her husband as " the deliverer of my country "—and were dashed as she remembered that he was " delivering " it from her father.

The two were crowned in April (1689), the Bishop of London officiating in place of the Archbishop of Canterbury who refused, announcing that James was still King. Nor would he give Mary his blessing although she sent to ask for it soon after her arrival in England, telling her that she must rather ask her father's, for it would not otherwise " be heard in Heaven."

Another who held aloof was Thomas Ken, once Mary's chaplain in Holland and now Bishop of Bath and Wells. During the debates in the Lords he had voted repeatedly against the throne being considered "vacant," and after his last useless protest had left Parliament for ever. Nor would he make any secret of his loyalty to James or attend Mary's Court.

But though bishops might disapprove, enthusiastic crowds thronged the streets to cheer and fling their hats into the air when

Garter-King-at-Arms made his usual proclamation at Whitehall and Temple Bar,
" followed by the Maces of both Houses and
the two Speakers."

It was only down quiet lanes that men
hummed :

> " All hail to the Orange—My Masters, come on,
> I'll tell you what wonders he for us has done.
>   He has pulled down the father and thrust out the son,
> And put by the daughters to fill up the throne with—
>   An Orange ! "

There could be no coronation in Scotland
as the regalia was being held for James, the
exiled King. A number of Scottish clans
openly proclaimed their refusal to swear
allegiance to the intruders from Holland, and
seventeen bold chieftains had put on paper
their scorn of the " usurpers "; but this did
not prevent commissioners from posting
down the North Road to offer the sove-
reignty of the ancient realm by " unanimous
vote."

So Mary and William, strong in the faith
of their mission, went their ways, living
laborious days and working in spheres that
were strictly masculine and feminine.

Mary was much shocked at the lack of
religion in the life of the people, " and they
so lately in imminent danger." It affected

herself too, and looking back over past weeks she found that when preparing for her coronation she had had scarce leisure " to go twice daily to public prayer," instead of four times.

Hoping to do some good she introduced Sunday afternoon sermons at Whitehall and never failed to attend; indeed she offered an example to the Court since she " listened without drowsiness."

Going further the sovereigns permitted their names to appear on a broadsheet issued " for the encouragement of Virtue and Good Living and the Discouragement of Vice," and became royal patrons of various " societies for the reformation of manners," to the members of which " all prophanesses what- ever " were strictly forbidden.

Incidentally, Mary superintended her wardrobe and checked her accounts, scrutin- ising such items as the charges for " putting a rich ermine mantle into a new outside," and the number of " choice squirral bellys " ordered for the lining of her " pettycoat."

She drank tea at three guineas a pound and grieved because she and her sister Anne were no longer close companions as in the days of their youth, though soon after her first coming to England Anne had christened yet a second little daughter after her restored

sister. Like the first she had died almost
immediately.

Later, Mary was to ask herself if the
estrangement was " God's punishment for
the irregularity committed by us upon the
revolution."

At the end of the first year's reign Mary
wrote her " customary reflections " in her
diary :

" . . . I am come to the crown and so
raised to the highest condition of human
life, but I don't look on it as such. . . . The
only thing that pleaseth me is the hope of
being, in time (together with my husband),
the instrument of good in God's hands. . . .

" When I look back on what I was last
year and think what I am now, it amazes
me to see how well I ended the last and how
ill I begin this. . . ."

The times were difficult and William decided to go to Ireland, whereupon Mary " fell
into a great melancholie " and roused herself
with an effort when her husband determined
to leave the control of affairs in her hands
during his absence. Mary begged that he
would so arrange things that she " might
not make a foolish figure in the world " while
he was away.

" My opinion having ever been that woman

should not meddle in government I have never given myself to be inquisitive in these kind of matters," she wrote forlornly when driven to attend a cabinet meeting. But when a crisis came she faced it bravely. It was not for nothing that the blood of the Stuarts ran in her veins mingled with that of Clarendon, lawyer and statesman ; the ghost of the little serving-maid who had boldly tramped the highways looking for work must have been proud of her descendant.

Three weeks after William's departure the French fleet appeared in the Channel and scored a success over the combined English and Dutch fleets. Mary, counting her husband's letters " all the comfort this world affords," wrote of her dread that " something may happen to prevent us hearing from you," but when news of the disaster at sea sent London into a panic she kept her head and proved herself every inch a Queen.

Reviewing her soldiers in Hyde Park she let no sign of anxiety appear, although she was so well aware of the seriousness of the position that she had ordered all cattle to be removed from the coast " in case the French should land."

But before the enemy could follow up his first success William had struck his blow

on the Boyne and Mary could write in her
diary :

" The Lord was pleased to do more for me
than I could hope, for he wonderfully pre-
served my husband, giving him a great
victory. . . . And He kept my father and
him far from each other . . . and me from
committing any fault. . . ."

But in the eyes of the stubborn few James
was still King.   The uncompromising Bishop
of Bath and Wells kept his flag flying, despite
his old friendship for Mary in the days when
she was Princess of Orange and William's
treatment of her had stirred his indignation.
" Madame," he wrote to her, " I do not
give you ye title of Majesty not daring to
do so, because I think it justly belongs to
none but your royal father and his queen."
Still, he struggled to believe that Mary had
been " misguided," rather than " wilfully
evil," and begged her to consider the duty
she owed to her father and brother as well
as her husband, these being " not at all in-
consistent. . . .   No one command of God
should be violated to gratify another, no evil
should be done to promote our most holy
religion—and there could be no true repen-
tance without restitution."
He added that he would willingly sacrifice

his life to heal such wounds as Mary had
given " to our conscience," and wished his
eyes " fountains of tears " to wash away the
sins of the late revolution.

" . . . God, out of ye multitude of His
tender mercies, give you grace to weep much,
to love much, and withal to be most beloved
of God," he ended.

But there is no proof that Mary received
the letter on which the good bishop had
spent much thought.

La Hogue was fought (1692) and James's
fate was sealed.

" God alone delivered us and I gave myself to joy," wrote Mary.

The rule of William and Mary was now
definitely established, but though the nation
accepted the position it would have no sailing under false colours and a veritable storm
of protest arose when Burnet, Bishop of
Salisbury, issued a pastoral letter in which
the power wielded by the House of Orange
was mentioned as being " exercised by right
of conquest."   Nor was the bishop alone in
his contention, for a book entitled *King William and Queen Mary, Conquerors,* was in
circulation.   The exasperated populace saw
to it that both these manifestations were
publicly burnt " by the common hangman."

" . . . I have had no such trials this year as I had last, neither of joy nor sorrow," wrote Mary, " but great reason to bless my God. . . . I have continued a pretty even course—though not so well as I could wish— but I have prayed more this year than last, both more frequently and more fervently . . . and thus in very good disposition of mind I bless my God and end the year 1693."

But the burden of the crown did not grow lighter for William was much away, and relations with Anne continued strained.

There came a day when Mary fell ill. The diagnosis varied. Now it was said that she had measles, and now scarlet fever. And then the whisper ran that the Queen had erysipelas. All were wrong ; Mary had contracted small-pox. Knowing it, she made her preparations ; William was near and she felt at peace.

Bishop Burnet came to give her Holy Communion, but Mary was so drowsy that she could hardly rouse herself to take the sacrament.

" Others have need to pray for me, seeing that I am so little able to pray for myself," she murmured.

Mary died in Christmas week and a wave of sorrow swept Holland for this " incomparable Queen." But in staunch Jacobite

circles there was no mourning and one stiff-
necked divine preached his Sunday sermon
from the text : " Go now, see this accursed
woman and bury her, for she is a King's
daughter."

There was a lying-in-state and a funeral
ceremony at which attended " all the Parliament men and 400 old women all having
new cloaks, and the streets were hung with
black."

The Bishop of Gloucester preached such
a sermon that he moved the congregation to
tears. " God saw her to be too good for a
people who would not mend in the least by
her example and so took her hence."

Knowing that the thoughts of many must
be with the exiled King he faced the subject
boldly and asked his hearers whether the
late Queen should have been " so wilful as
to prefer the false interest of a father to
both the spiritual and temporal interest of
the whole nation ? "

She would then indeed have left a " blot on
her now spotless and most precious memory,"
he told them.

As for her attributes as a wife,

" she had spent so little that it was inad-
visable to say what she had laid out on her
apparel. . . . And what an enemy she was
to idleness even in ladies ! . . . In the last

place," he ended, " I cannot forbear taking notice of another rare endowment with which her majesty was adorned and one which few would expect to find in the character of a woman though a queen—courage and fortitude ! . . ."

A woman who had been close to the Queen wrote :

" God has been pleased to shorten her days as a reward for her sufferings which were not slight, and which, with the goodness of her own nature, had formed in her so great a degree of virtue that it might truly be said the world was not worthy of her."

A man saw her from a different angle :

" In sum she was such an admirable woman, (abating for taking the crown without more due apology,) as does, if possible, outshine the renouned Elizabeth."

CHAPTER VIII

" THE MILDEST AND MEEKEST OF HER SEX "

1723–1772

MARY PRINCESS OF ENGLAND, LANDGRAVINE OF HESSE-CASSEL

Born	.	.	.	. February 22, 1723
Married	.	.	.	. May 8, 1740
Died .	.	.	.	. June 14, 1772

Descent

James I (VI of Scotland) *m.* Anne of Denmark
|
Elizabeth (and others)
m. Frederic V, Prince Palatine, and became Queen of Bohemia
|
Sophia (and others)
m. Ernest Augustus and became Electress of Hanover
|
George I (and others)
|
George II (and another)
m. Caroline of Anspach
|
Mary (and others)
m. Frederick, afterwards Landgrave of Hesse-Cassel
Left surviving children

CHAPTER VIII

"THE MILDEST AND GENTLEST OF HER SEX"

EIGHTEENTH CENTURY

" POOR Caroline, it is a fine legacy I leave
you—the trouble of educating these two
young things!" said the dying Queen of
George II to an elder daughter, for Mary
and Louisa were only fourteen and thirteen
years of age, and their mother saw little
prospect for them in the future when they
became dependent upon their brother.

To avoid such a fate Anne, Princess Royal
and eldest of the five sisters, had been
willing to make any marriage that offered.
At sixteen, she had hoped for the King of
France, and when the tentative offer was
declined by her parents on religious grounds
had waited impatiently while the years
slipped by and she passed her twenty-fourth
milestone.

A proposal from Holland opened the way
for Anne to follow in the footsteps of two
other English Princesses and marry the
Prince of Orange.

" I do not care how ugly he may be, I would marry him were he a Dutch baboon ! " she exclaimed, waving aside warnings.

The bridegroom arrived and Anne's behaviour was " something marvellous for propriety." Friendly onlookers described his countenance as " far from disagreeable," those more critical considered his " body as bad as possible." Lord Chesterfield admitted that " the prince's shape was not so advantageous as it should be," but added that he was " perfectly well-bred and civil to everybody."

Amelia, the second daughter in George's large family, vowed that *she* could never have accepted such a man, but Caroline thought Anne " wise."

The little sisters Mary and Louisa were discreetly silent, but they doubtless watched open-eyed when, after the midnight wedding ceremony, the Court attended the bridal couple as they took their places in the state bed, Anne's pox-marks unusually vivid and the Prince's night attire of silver tissue and peruke cruelly emphasising his wry neck and deformity of figure.

Lord Hervey did his best to comfort the Queen by assuring her that " in half a year all persons look alike," and Anne would no longer notice her husband's peculiarities.

MARY, DAUGHTER OF GEORGE II AND QUEEN CAROLINE, LATER PRINCESS OF HESSE-CASSEL.

From a picture at Windsor.   By gracious permission of His Majesty the King.

" The figure of the body one's married grows so familiar to the eye that one looks at it mechanically," he explained.

The next marriage in the family was that of Frederick Prince of Wales and it occasioned a fine family dispute, for when his sisters came to dine with the Prince and his fiancée the day before the ceremony, Frederick decreed that rigid Court etiquette should be enforced and they must sit on " stools, not chairs."

The affronted Princesses stood upon their dignity and declined to enter the dining-room until the offending seats were removed !

After an interlude came a proposal for Mary, which, if peacefully contemplated by the family, brought dissension into the Cabinet.

The King, impatient to be off to the Hanover he loved, made a brief announcement to the effect that the marriage of his fourth daughter to Prince Frederick of Hesse, son of the Landgrave, would take place a few days later, whereupon the Archbishop of Canterbury and the Bishop of London each claimed the honour of performing the ceremony and the Cabinet promptly divided.

Another difficulty arose as to whether

Mary should be actually married or merely
" contracted by solemn espousals."

The original plan had been that Prince
Frederick should come to England and
marry the Princess in person, but George had
vetoed the scheme on the ground of expense
—he had no wish to lavish entertainment
on a son-in-law—hence the problem.

The representatives of the Church united
in objecting to a marriage by proxy, for which
there had been no precedent since ,the
Reformation, but George opposed them.   It
was beneath his dignity to send his daughter
to a man who when she arrived " had it in
his power to call her his wife or not,"
therefore Mary must be firmly married
before she sailed.   In the end the ecclesiastics
gave way, " as these, when they give up no
power or profit, are not addicted to being
very stiff in their opposition to the will of
the court."

Now it was the turn of the judiciary.
Legal lights pointed out that if Mary were
married by proxy it might jeopardise the
right of succession of her children to the
throne, should she have any—and those
more remote than Mary's unborn infants
had inherited the crown of England before
now.   Did not the Act of Succession stipulate
that the marriage of a member of the royal

family performed in England must be
according to the form of the Anglican
Church ? and that form, by virtue of the
Act of Uniformity, was the service for Holy
Matrimony in the Book of Common Prayer.

Why had not Sir Robert Walpole explained
this to his Majesty ? Badgered Sir Robert
explained that he had done so that very
morning, "and the King had replied, I will
hear no more of your church nonsense, nor
your law nonsense. . . . I will have my
daughter married here and I will have the
marriage complete ! "

There seemed no way out of the *impasse*
till one more learned than the rest turned
back the pages of history and persuaded the
irate King, now chafing on the leash and
believing all were in league to detain him
from Hanover, that what a former Princess
Mary could do, might be permitted to a
modern maiden " without loss or damage."
Tired of the subject George decided to be as
acquiescent as Henry VIII. This agreement
settled the Church dispute too, for the
Secretary of State and not an ecclesiastic
officiated at proxy espousals, while the Archbishop of Canterbury would offer up the
prayers.

Two days later the ceremony took place,
the Duke of Cumberland acting as proxy

bridegroom.   Directed by the Duke of New-
castle he took the Princess Mary by the
right hand and recited :

" The most serene Prince, Frederick of
Hesse-Cassel, doth by me, William Duke of
Cumberland, duly authorised and appointed
for this purpose . . . take thee, Princess
Mary, to be his wedded wife, to have and to
hold, from this day forward, for better for
worse, for richer for poorer, in sickness and
health, to love and to cherish till Death
doth him and you part according to God's
Holy Ordinance, and hereby he plights thee
his Troth by me, by Virtue of the said
Letters of Procuration "

Mary, a seventeen-year-old bride and
" handsome enough to be an artist's model,"
made the answering vows :

" I, Mary, do by you, William Duke of
Cumberland, duly authorised and appointed
for this purpose . . . take the most Serene
Prince Frederick of Hesse-Cassel to be my
wedded Husband. . . ."

A contract was signed, after which " His
Royal Highness the Duke did, in the name
of the most Serene Prince Frederick, put a
ring on the 4th finger of Princess Mary's
left hand " which Mary accepted from the

Serene Frederick " as delivered to me by
you, William Duke of Cumberland."

And now the Archbishop of Canterbury
delivered his Latin discourse and benediction, praying that " God would direct to
temporal and eternal welfare the two
illustrious princes just espoused."

He pointed out that at weddings it was
customary to speculate upon the future of
the bride and bridegroom,

" which custom . . . we are persuaded to
follow at this time, not only by the eminent
virtues of this magnanimous Youth, whereof
we have heard by Fame, but by that modesty
so conspicuous in the behaviour of the Royal
Virgin. . . . As for the advantages of her
Person (though these also are excellent and
attract the Eyes of all), we say nothing.
. . . Matters of greater importance call for
our attention. . . ."

Having offered congratulations " in the
name of the rest of our fellow subjects
present and those who sorely regret their
absence," the tactful Archbishop turned his
attention to George II.

" O, King of Monarchs ! the Father, Glory
and Pillar of our country, with grateful
hearts we render thee thanks that without
thinking it a diminution, or foreign to that

High Dignity to which the Disposer of all
Things has . . . advanced your majesty,
you are always watching diligently for our
safety, and that even in your private family
(if it may be allowed to call anything private
which concerns so great a King) you don't
suffer anything to be done but what may
tend to the good of the Public ! "

There were more ceremonies before Mary
was sent to her husband, and in these too
the King was not forgotten. It was to him
the Lord Mayor and Aldermen went first
to offer their congratulatory address " on
this, which happy event your loyal subjects
consider as a farther instance of your
majesty's steady attention to the honour
and interest of your crown. . . .

" May God grant," added the loyal
representative of the City of London, " that
your royal house may forever supply the
great Protestant Families of Europe with
such invaluable blessings as are now secured
to his Serene Highness the Prince of Hesse,
by the going forth of this Royal Progeny
who had been formed by Religion and
Virtue on the illustrious pattern set by
your majesty. . . ."

George accepted the dutiful congratulations, ignored the compliments and permitted
his hand to be kissed.

The Lord Mayor and his Aldermen now waited upon Mary to mention that she was about to meet a Prince who was " impatiently waiting to receive a consort emulating the virtues of her royal parents." Though Great Britain was " by degrees being deprived of her daughters, yet it was a consolation to the kingdom to see them so deservedly placed at the head of the most considerable Protestant families in Europe."

" I am thankful to you for your congratulations upon this occasion," said Mary making the only speech of hers which has been recorded. " You may be assured of my sincerest wishes for the Welfare and Prosperity of the City of London."

She sailed, to be met in her new country " with all possible marks of Joy and Affection," but Frederick of Hesse-Cassel proved anything but " serene " and was not a " Magnanimous Youth " ; Mary became known as " the unhappy Princess of Hesse."

Walpole described him as " tall, lusty and handsome. I daresay in his own country he is reckoned very lively, for though he don't speak much he opens his mouth very often." A less friendly observer found the Prince " an obstinate, illiterate and ill-tempered German boor," even though, later, he hired out his Hessian troops to assist

in the war against the " North American
Colonies."

Mary's happiest times were those when
she could escape to Bath on the pretence
of drinking the waters, and visit her elder
sister Caroline, " who loved her extremely."

Perhaps, even though Mary had " the
softest mildest temper in the world," she
was stirred to tell the Princess Louisa
something of the truth, for when, a few
years after Mary's disastrous matrimonial
venture, this younger sister married the
King of Denmark, she vowed that, come
what may, none of her relatives should be
allowed to know if she too were unhappy.

After fourteen years of life with Frederick
Mary found freedom in a separation when
the Prince became a convert to Roman
Catholicism. She retreated to Hanau with
her children, finding a friend in her father-
in-law who carried her into safety when
French troops overran the principality in
the course of a war with Prussia.

A frantic message to England told of
Mary's need ; she was " lodged at an inn
without provision for a table."   Parliament
was not sitting but Pitt sent her £20,000 on
his own responsibility and saw to it that she
received an income.

The death of Mary's father-in-law forced

her into public office. She became Regent of Hanau and developed some of her mother's capacity for administration.

Her death disturbed London society, for though she had been " long ill and never happy " the end came unexpectedly and the best people were unable to attend the opening of the Pantheon " for lack of mourning."

Contemporaries described the dead Princess as " a gentle, amiable being," who had been treated by her husband " with a degree of inhumanity only exceeded by the unrepining gentleness with which she had endured his incessant brutalities."

CHAPTER IX
THE " SWEET " PRINCESS
1776–1857

MARY PRINCESS OF ENGLAND AND DUCHESS OF GLOUCESTER

Born	.	.	.	. April 25, 1776
Married	.	.	.	. July 22/23, 1816
Died .	.	.	.	. April 30, 1857

Descent

James I (VI of Scotland) *m.* Anne of Denmark
|
Elizabeth (and others)
m. Frederic V, Prince Palatine, and became
Queen of Bohemia
|
Sophia (and others)
m. Ernest Augustus and became Electress of Hanover
|
George I (and others)
m. Sophia Dorothea of Celle
|
George II (and another)
m. Caroline of Anspach
|
George III (grandson of George II)
m. Charlotte of Mecklenburgh-Strelitz
|
Mary (and others)
m. William Frederick, Duke of Gloucester

CHAPTER IX

THE "SWEET" PRINCESS

WHEN George Augustus Frederick, eldest son of George III and Queen Charlotte, was born he was put on view daily " from 1 p.m. till 3 p.m.," but by the time Mary came to find a place in the crowded royal nurseries the birth of a new prince or princess hardly caused a ripple on the surface of society.

Kew was a favourite residence while the children were young, and here etiquette was less rigidly enforced than at Windsor where the little people were never permitted to forget that their parents were sovereign monarchs nor to speak until addressed by the King or Queen.

But wherever the Court was in residence George and Charlotte gave watchful attention to their family. They rose early and at 8 a.m. the elder sons and daughters made their punctual appearance to spend an hour with their parents before the little ones appeared "to lisp or smile their goodmorrows," when their seniors settled down to serious study.

Once a week the King and Queen " attended by their whole offspring in pairs " made a tour of Richmond Gardens, when the loyal citizens thronged to admire the ten little Princes and Princesses so paraded, and were pleased to note that " parental partiality seems unknown at Court."

There may have been little favouritism, but there was certainly plenty of discipline so far as the boys were concerned, for the King was a firm believer in the old adage, " Spare the rod and spoil the child," particularly as regarded his elder sons.

" If they deserve it, let them be flogged," were the orders given to the tutors. " Do as you used to do at Westminster." And once, at least, as their sisters wept, the furious Princes were held by attendants and whipped under the King's eyes.

Perhaps the Prince of Wales and the Duke of York envied their younger brother Clarence, who was sent to sea at thirteen and served as a midshipman under Nelson.

If the Princesses were not subjected to corporal punishment they experienced a certain amount of mental discipline.

There is a nursery story of Mary, aged six, in tears over a difficult lesson :

MARY, DAUGHTER OF GEORGE III AND QUEEN CHARLOTTE, AFTERWARDS DUCHESS OF GLOUCESTER.

From a picture by Hoppner at Windsor. By gracious permission of His Majesty the King.

" I cannot comprehend it, madame ! I cannot comprehend it ! " sobbed the little Princess to the Queen.

" What you cannot comprehend to-day, you may comprehend to-morrow," said Charlotte serenely, or so the tale runs, " and what you cannot attain to this year, you may next. Do not, therefore, be frightened of little difficulties, but attend to what you know. . . ."

At Windsor, life was as carefully ordered and hardly less quiet than at Kew. With the family following in a school-like " crocodile " the King and Queen would lead the way to early morning prayers in the Chapel, then came breakfast when " all the sweet princesses " would listen with serious attention did the King deign to read aloud from the newspapers such items as he thought suited to the female intelligence. In the evening the family met again, card tables were set out and those of " the sweet princesses " who were of a suitable age attended on their mother. They were not allowed to sit in her presence without express permission and sometimes one would fall asleep behind her chair.

But whatever the effects of the royal method of upbringing on the sons, Queen Charlotte's daughters won golden opinions from those who came in contact with them.

"Amazingly well are all these children brought up," said Miss Burney, captivated by Princess Mary who, " capering upstairs," stopped short instantly at the sight of a stranger, " becoming demure and asking me how I did with all the composure of a woman of mature years."

At four years of age Mary was seen as " a sweet child in cherry-coloured tabby with silver leading strings : ' How do you do, Duchess of Portland's friend ? ' she said, sweeping a deep curtsey, undismayed at having forgotten the name of the lady to whom she was speaking."

But the great festivals at Windsor were birthdays. There would be " new frocks for everyone," and "sumptuous dinners and desserts." All the officers and ladies of the Court came to offer their compliments to the heroine of the occasion, and, weather permitting, the entire royal family would walk on the terrace, the owner of the birth-day leading the way through the avenue of admiring people, then the King and Queen, and finally the remaining Princesses " in due position according to age," each with her own lady-in-waiting, and all sweeping deep curtseys to those they wished to honour.

" Never were six sister princesses so

lovely ! " And never can the old walls of
Windsor have looked down on a more
charming scene.

To these six little Princesses the children
of England owe a debt of gratitude, since the
first Christmas tree in England was lighted
for their benefit ; Queen Charlotte had loved
the pretty custom in the days when she was
a cinderella princess in Mecklenburgh-Strelitz ! [1]

Music was a favourite study. Handel's
harpsicord stood in the simply furnished
rooms and he gave lessons at Court. Elizabeth and " the sweet Princess Mary " used to
sing part-songs together " very prettily in
point of voice. Their good humour, however, inherent condescension and sweetness
of manner would make a much worse performance pleasing," was the verdict of one
auditor, but Mrs. Delany, with whom the
Princesses Elizabeth, Mary and Sophia once
breakfasted, was more appreciative.

" I entreated Princess Mary to play the
lesson of Handel and she, with all the sweetness in the world, played it twice ! . . . Then
she and Princess Sophia sang the Hallelujah
Chorus in the Messiah. . . . Mary has a fine
voice . . . and they looked like little angels !

[1] See *Her Majesty : The Romance of the Queens of England.*

. . . They are very, *very* fair, with blue eyes
and a vast deal of hair which curls down
their backs. . . . They go without caps and
are so engaging in behaviour that everyone
loves them and admires those that made
them what they are."

Being one of the youngest members of a
very large family, the intimate tragedies that
affected her elder sisters left Princess Mary
untouched. She could sleep quietly behind
her white dimity bedcurtains while her elders
hovered in constant attendance on the Queen,
who was afraid to be left alone with the
King, and if she realised the nature of her
father's illness it was probably blotted from
her mind by the interest of the journey to
Weymouth, where the family went for the
King's convalescence, the journey being
broken en route for a brief stay in the New
Forest, where Mary met her cousin Prince
William, son of the Duke of Gloucester.

At fifteen the Princess made her début at
a Birthday Ball at St. James's in a fever of
anxiety as to the management of her hoop
and train !

The Duke of Clarence, home from the sea,
was to have danced with her but he, having
drunk the King's health, must needs drink
a second to the Queen and became " very

merry," so merry that he could not partner his sister !

" You may think how far gone I was for I kissed Schwellenberg's hand," he explained later when excusing his absence.

However, despite her disappointment Princess Mary looked " interesting and most unaffectedly lovely," according to Miss Burney. Another onlooker described her as " a sweet creature and perhaps in point of beauty the first of this truly beautiful race . . . she might well be called the pendant to the Prince of Wales."

Family troubles grew worse. Knowledge of the Prince's escapades could not be kept from his sisters, despite the Queen's rigid ideas as to the carefully nurtured life that her daughters should lead. Now he was most woefully in debt; now the bailiffs were in his house; now people whispered of " Mrs. Prince."

The Princess Royal effected her escape by marrying. A fanatic shot at the King in the presence of the Queen and his daughters. Princess Amelia died, but the remaining sisters still attended on their mother, played cards, drew or knitted night after night as they sat around a table ostensibly listening to " improving " reading.

But Mary remained " all good humour

and pleasantness, her manners perfect !—
I never saw or conversed with any princess
so exactly what she ought to be," said Lord
Malmesbury.

But the years passed and youth slipped by.
And now the Prince of Wales was Regent,
King in all but name, and he brought about
the emancipation of his sisters, moving the
House of Commons to "make such provision for them as if the King were actually
defunct."

Four years later Mary came into temporary
limelight, for the Prince Regent mentioned
her in a speech from the throne in the House
of Lords.

"I have given the Royal Consent to a
marriage between his majesty's daughter,
Princess Mary, and the Duke of Gloucester,
and am persuaded that this event will be
highly gratifying to his majesty's subjects."

It was, and the popular press of the day
expressed the view of the people :

"Never was union more calculated to
produce happiness to the parties and entire
satisfaction to the nation."

The Duke was the Prince William Mary
had met in the New Forest, who had now
succeeded to his father's title.   "His Royal

Highness is well-known as a liberal patron of almost every useful and charitable establishment in the Empire," wrote the social correspondents, " while the Princess, as is most fitted to her sex, is hardly known out of the domestic circle." The marriage of this " highly respectable pair, reckoned by their manners and principles peculiarly fitted for the duties of domestic life," it seemed, had been delayed, officially owing to the absence of the Duke of Cambridge, actually until Mary's niece Princess Charlotte had been safely wedded.

Now invitations were sent out and " the Queen's Palace was fitted up for the performance of the nuptial ceremony," which took place in the evening, according to the fashion of the day.

The Duke visited his fiancée in the morning, " seeing her in the presence of the Queen and all the princesses," and then returned to Gloucester House. Nothing more happened until seven o'clock that night when a guard-of-honour marched into the courtyard and guests began to arrive.

The bride was dressed " with her usual beautiful simplicity." A bandeau of white roses fastened together with sprigs of pearls is the only article of attire mentioned,— but, " the prevailing shade was blue."

" At 1/4 past nine guns were fired as a signal that the ceremony was over and at 10 p.m. the newly married pair drove off to Bagshot."

Six months later, Miss Burney, now Madame D'Arblay, paying a visit to Court, met " My sweet Duchess of Gloucester " with the Duke; he, it seemed, was "well-bred, polite, easy, unassuming, kind and not condescending."

Waterloo had been fought a year before, continental customers had been lost, bad weather had ruined the crops, and times were difficult. Wages had been reduced, factories stood idle, thousands of men were unemployed and subscription lists had to be opened to help the hard-hit workers and colliers who came marching to the cities to demonstrate their need and call public attention to their plight. In Merthyr Tydfil and other Welsh towns the military had to be called out to quell disturbances. So, when it was announced that " the establishment of the Duke and Duchess of Gloucester was to be framed on a scale of moderation which rendered unnecessary any application to the public purse " there was general relief.

Mary was forty and married, but marriage proved no more exciting than her long spinsterhood. She took small part in her husband's public life and still remained her mother's daughter.

When the Queen lay dying it was Mary who thought to send word to Madame D'Arblay, and when the erstwhile Court attendant wrote to her after Charlotte's death the Duchess " deigned to answer " the very moment she received the letter.

" I was touched to the heart," says Madame D'Arblay.

Unassisted by Mary the Duke fought for the abolition of slavery, voted for the repeal of an act which made " stealing privately in shops to the value of five shillings " a capital offence, and when a petition was presented to Parliament urging that Dissenters should be permitted to take degrees at Cambridge, he, as Chancellor, denounced the Bill most vigorously, contending that its promoters had " mistaken the intention of the pious founders who intended universities for the education of members of the Church."

But, unfortunately for the Duchess, public life did not exhaust the energies of " Silly Billy," as some had dared to nickname the Duke, and Mary found herself still under tutelage.

As a housewife, this daughter of Queen Charlotte proved a failure.

On one occasion, a lady wishing to pay her respects to the Duchess found herself conducted to the attic floor of the Park Lane house, where the Princess Mary met her breathless visitor to explain that the Duke had locked the drawing-room suite and taken away the key, since he was " discontent " at the state in which the apartment was kept !

Eighteen years of matrimony left Mary ailing, and when the Duke died it was whispered that " although his amiability had endeared him to a large circle by whom he will be sincerely lamented," the Duchess might take on a new lease of life, since " there is nothing so bad for the health as small daily worries, and nothing so trying as ennui."

The seers were right.   Princess Mary grew well and once again joined the Court circle and sat knitting at a table.   William IV was King now, and Adelaide was Queen.[1]

William died and the Duchess of Gloucester saw her young niece Victoria crowned.

It was to her sympathetic ear that the

[1] See *Her Majesty : The Romance of the Queens of England.*

Queen confessed that "proposing to dear Albert was a nervous thing to do," though necessary because "he would never have presumed to take such a liberty."

Princess Mary sponsored Victoria's first child and almost lived to see her god-child married.

"We all looked upon her as a kind of grandmother," wrote the Queen in her diary when the Duchess died at her house in Park Lane at the end of April 1857.

CHAPTER X

" OUR " PRINCESS
"LA BELLE ROSE ANGLAISE"

PRESENT TIME

H.R.H. PRINCESS MARY, VISCOUNTESS LASCELLES

Born (York Cottage, Sandringham) · · · · · April 25, 1897

Married (at Westminster Abbey) · · · · · February 28, 1922

Descent

George III *m.* Charlotte of Mecklenburgh-Strelitz

Edward Duke of Kent *m.* Victoria, dr. of Duke of Saxe-Coburg

Adolphus Duke of Cambridge *m.* Augusta, dr. of Landgrave of Hesse (and others)

Victoria *m.* Albert of Coburg and Gotha

Mary Adelaide (and others) *m.* Francis Duke of Teck

Edward-VII (and others) *m.* Alexandra of Denmark

George V (and others) *m.* Victoria Mary (and others)

Princess Mary (and others)

CHAPTER X

" OUR " PRINCESS
"LA BELLE ROSE ANGLAISE"

NINETEENTH AND TWENTIETH CENTURIES.

A HUNDRED and twenty-one years separated the birth of Princess Mary, daughter of George V and Queen Mary, from that of her immediate predecessor Princess Mary, daughter of George III and Queen Charlotte, but, oddly enough, both were April babies and share the 25th of that month as a birthday.

" Our " Princess narrowly escaped being called " Diamond " to celebrate the fact that she was born in the year of Queen Victoria's Jubilee ; as it is, it is only because she is known to the world as " Princess Mary " that it is possible to include her in a book of " Royal Marys," for her first names are Victoria, Alexandra and Alice.

As a baby she was very fair with blue eyes, tossed fair curls and soft flushed cheeks. " Oh, *la belle rose anglaise!* " cried a French visitor seeing her for the first time, and those around thought the pretty name well bestowed.

One girl in a family of boys soon develops the maternal instinct and this little Princess was no exception to the rule :

" Never mind, *I* will take good care of us," she promised, clinging comfortingly to her mother when, as Duchess of York, our present Queen was leaving England with the Duke on a long colonial tour.

Princess Mary's education began early. In order to give her the companionship of girls of her own age, several children whose parents were known to the Queen shared the Princess's lessons. In addition she attended a drill class at a well-known gymnasium, and danced, cycled and rode with her brothers, being given a pony " of her very own " as soon as she had learnt to be safe in the saddle.

The Princess was taught thrift by being encouraged to open a Savings Bank account, and from this she could draw what money she liked to go shopping and buy " surprise " presents.

Every girl should know how to mend, thought the Queen, so Princess Mary can darn. She was taught to cook, and in childhood delighted in making butter in the cool dairy at Sandringham. She can sew— some of the first garments contributed by her to the Queen's Needlework Guild were sprinkled with tears, for needles in unprac-

[*Vandyk.*

H.R.H. PRINCESS MARY.

226]

tised childish hands are liable to make sur-
prisingly large stitches and the work of a
princess, however small, passes under critical
eyes. In later years these contributions—
into which she could put personal service,
sure that what she made was going to be
used by people living the everyday life that
looks so strangely romantic to one obliged
to live forever in the glare of publicity—
became a very real pleasure.

Princess Mary's first formal public appearance was at the coronation of the King and
Queen. Wearing pale blue velvet robes
with an ermine train, and a coronet on her
fair hair, she drove through the crowded
streets to Westminster Abbey sitting beside
the Prince of Wales, her younger brothers
facing her.

A year later, the world still unshadowed
by the Great War, came the joy of a first
visit abroad when she went with the Queen
to Germany. She thought it would be the
first of many such tours and would have been
amazed could anyone have told her that the
next time she crossed the Channel it would be
to carry a message from the Queen to women
workers in the war zone of a stricken country.

In 1914 Princess Mary was in the most
impressionable stage of her girlhood, but not

even for a King's daughter, and she " all the daughters of her father's house," could there be care-free days in that or the ensuing years.

Like every girl in the kingdom Princess Mary was eager to do something practical, something that would show her vivid personal interest in the rank and file of those who were carrying the burden of the war, so just before that first dark Christmas she sent out an appeal asking the nation to help her to send a present to every sailor on the high seas and every soldier on the fields of battle.

The response was immediate and a hundred thousand pounds flowed in. Millions of brass boxes were dispatched, each containing tobacco, cigarettes or chocolate, each emblazoned with Princess Mary's portrait and containing a card from her " and friends at home," wishing the recipient a " Happy Christmas and a Victorious New Year."

But the " Victorious New Year " did not come. England grew darker and princes, princess and people more eager for work.

Always the Princess had wished to be closer to " ordinary " life, to live and help as might others of her age, unweighted by royal rank instead of being obliged to stand a little aloof, and to a certain degree the war helped her, since it showed her a more intimate side of life than falls to the lot of most princesses. Her blue eyes learned to look on tragic sights.

As a King's daughter, in times of peace she might have gone with the Queen to open bazaars and fetes; as it was she followed her mother down interminable hospital wards and paused by the bedsides of wounded and maimed men.

Our island home is small and crowded; people began to fear hunger. Princess Mary went with the Queen to open municipal kitchens.

Women and girls were taking up all manner of work and everything they did claimed the Princess's attention, making a direct human call upon her young energies.

When the Court was at Windsor she did canteen work at the nearest munition factory, and when a Voluntary Aid Detachment was formed at Buckingham Palace Princess Mary, as eagerly as every other girl whose brother, cousins and friends were at the front, went to listen to lectures on First Aid and struggle with the intricacies of bandaging.

Her coming-of-age gift was the strangest ever given to a King's daughter. It was permission to go as a probationer to the Hospital for Sick Children, Great Ormond Street.

" Is she a real Princess ? " doubting children would ask, seeing her in nursing uniform.

" Has Princess Mary been looking after *my* child ? " was many a mother's query.

After some experience on the medical side of the hospital the new probationer was transferred to the surgical side, and steadfast, if white, took her turn in the operating theatre. Other girls were doing this, and worse—why not she ?

This same year Princess Mary took military rank, for the King appointed her Colonel-in-Chief of the Royal Scots, that famous regiment which is in lineal descent from the romantic Scottish Guards who served the Kings of France.

When men of the Royal Scots returned home from captivity they found the Princess waiting to greet them and listen, wide-eyed, to the tragic stories they had to tell.

She grew eager and yet more eager to see the sites made famous by the valour of men, but Authority said that no princess might go to France till the guns ceased fire.

Armistice was signed and she sailed immediately to carry a message from the Queen to the women war-workers who had helped to bear the burden of the day across the Channel.

In her V.A.D. uniform Princess Mary took the salute of her own regiment as it marched through the streets of ruined Ypres, where a hundred thousand men had died. She saw the camouflaged roads, the duck-board trenches, the dead being collected from the battlefields, for war was still very near; almost, one could hear the long roll of the guns. Flanders poppies were not yet flowering in Flanders fields, but slender bulrushes were springing up from the water-logged shell-holes among the débris of war.

Peace had come, but the girlhood of the nation was awake and eager to be ready to undertake whatsoever burdens should be laid on the shoulders of the new generation, so Princess Mary became President of the Girl Guides, her one regret that once again her work must be at the top where it is lonely.—If only she could have a company of her very own !

The world began to recover. Landworkers, W.A.A.C.'s, "Wrens," all slipped out of uniform, and a nation, wishful to forget the tragic years, asked new duties from the King's daughter.

Sandbags were taken down, the lights of London went up, and Princess Mary "came out." Three years later her engagement was announced and good wishes poured in from the ends of the world, for never a princess in all the long line of Royal Marys had stood closer to the life of the people.

The wedding day came as it should have done, in sunshine, and the people were early astir. At last, after years of gloom, was a legitimate cause for care-free rejoicing.

For two hours before " the most English Princess " was due to leave Buckingham Palace the close-packed thousands cheered themselves hoarse and the excited roar could be heard in Piccadilly.

She came, a fairy Princess agleam with pearls (a rope had been threaded for her from the Marys of the Nation) and girdled with silver, riding in a golden coach, looking " just as a girl ought to look when she goes to her wedding," as the eager people told one another.

The ceremony in the Abbey was short. " Beloved, let us love one another," sang a boy's clear treble as the bride walked up the aisle towards the waiting bridegroom ; and the Archbishop of Canterbury spoke to her as " my child " when he gave the benediction and wished her " godspeed."

But one and all were too near sorrow to forget the war years completely, even for an hour. When Princess Mary drove down

Whitehall she stopped to lay flowers from her wedding bouquet at the Cenotaph.

Hand in hand with Viscount Lascelles she came out on to the balcony at Buckingham Palace to let the people see her, then, showered with rose-leaves and tiny silver horseshoes, drove away through the crowded streets, and all " wished her joy."

That night a message came to us all from the King :

" . . . The Queen and I cannot allow a day to pass which has been so happy and memorable, without making it known how deeply we have been touched by the warm and affectionate good wishes of our subjects in all parts of the Empire. . . . From the depths of our hearts we thank you for making yourselves partners in our joy. . . ."

" We wish her happiness," said the tired people.   " We wish her happiness ! "

BIBLIOGRAPHY

BIBLIOGRAPHY

NOTE.—Grateful thanks are due to the many authors whose works are named below, for unless those much wiser than I had made these careful and interesting records I could never have had the pleasure of writing *Royal Marys*.

My only regret is that it has not been possible to give chapter and verse for the many quotations I could not refrain from using.

E. THORNTON COOK.

Anecdotes, Dr. King's.
An Official Inaccuracy (C. J. Lemuer).
Archæologia (Society of Antiquaries. Vol. XVIII).
Aristocracy, Romance of the (Sir Bernard Burke).
Bath under Beau Nash (Lewis Melville).
Biography, Dictionary of National.
Boleyn, Life of Anne (Philip W. Sergeant).
Britain, Dalrymple's Memoirs of Great.
Buckingham Palace, The Story of (Bruce Graeme).
Calais, The Chronicle of (Ed. by J. G. Nichols (Camden Society)).
Charles I, Court and Times of (Gamache).
Charlotte, Court and Private Life in the Time of Queen (Mrs. Papendiek).
Cheque Book of the Royal Chapels (Dr. Rimbault (Camden Society)).
Chesterfield's Life and Letters.
Clarendon, Life of (By Himself).
Creevey Papers, The (Ed. by Sir Herbert Maxwell).

Croker, Correspondence and Diaries of the Right Hon. J. W.

D'Arblay, Diary and Letters of Madame.

Ecclesiastical Memorials (Strype).

Edward VI, Journal of.

Edward VI, Literary Remains of (Ed. by Nicolas (Roxburgh Club)).

Edward and Mary (Tytler).

Elizabeth, The Court of Queen (Lucy Aikin).

Elizabeth, The Girlhood of Queen (Frank A. Mumby).

Elizabeth of York, Memoir of (N. Harris Nicolas).

Elizabeth of York, Privy Purse Expenses of (N. Harris Nicolas).

Ellis's Original Letters.

English Princes, Memoirs of (W. H. Davenport Adams).

English Queens and Philip, Two (Martin Hume).

England, A Chronicle of (Ch. Wriothesley).

England, Gardiner's History of.

England, History of (Froude).

England, History of (Macaulay).

England, History of the Church of (Richard Watson Dixon).

England, Lingard's History of.

England, Lives of the Princesses of (Mrs. Everett Green).

England, Memoirs of the Court of (J. Heneage Jesse).

England, Parliamentary History of.

England, Queens of, of the House of Hanover (Dr. Doran).

England under the House of Hanover (Wright).

Evelyn's Diary.

Feria, Life of Jane Dormer, Duchess of (Henry Clifford. Ed. by Stevenson).

Froissart, Chronicles of (Ed. by Berners).

Fuller's Worthies.

Gentleman's Magazine.

George II, Memoirs of the Reign of (John, Lord Hervey).

George III, Journal of the Reign of (Walpole).

George III, Memoirs of the Court and Cabinet of (Duke of Buckingham).

George III, Memoirs of the Life and Reign of (J. Heneage Jesse).

George III, Memoirs of the Reign of (William Belsham).

Gloucester, Henry, Duke of, and the Princess of Orange, A Short View of the Lives of Those Illustrious Princes. Collected by T.M. to whom the same will serve as a Rule and Pattern.

Granville, Autobiography of Mary (Mrs. Delany).

Grenville Correspondence, The.

Hainault, Philippa of, and Her Times (B. C. Hardy).

Hall's Chronicles.

Henry VIII, Privy Purse Expenses of (N. H. Nicolas).

Historical Memoirs of My Own Times (Sir N. W. Wraxall).

Historical Tracts, Somers's.

History, Cambridge Modern.

History of His Own Times (Burnet).

History, Sandford's Genealogical.

Holinshed.

James II and his Wives (Allan Fea).

James, Life of (Rev. J. S. Clarke).

Jane and Queen Mary, Chronicles of Queen (Camden Society).

Ken, Life of (Plumptre).

Lake, Diary of Doctor (Ed. by G. P. Elliott (Camden Society)).

Leland's Collectanea.

Lieven and Earl Grey, Correspondence of the Princess.

London (Knight).

London Magazine and Monthly Chronologer, The.
Lords, Journals of the House of.
Machyn's Diary.
Malmesbury's Memoirs of an Ex-Minister, Lord.
Mary, On the Life and Death of Queen (E. Fowler).
Mary, Privy Purse Expenses of Princess (Memoir by
    Sir F. Madden).
Mary, The Accession of Queen (Antonio de Guaras.
    Tr. by Richard Garnett).
Mary I, History of (J. M. Stone).
Mary, Queen of England, Memoirs of (Ed. by Dr.
    Doebner).
Mary II (Mary F. Sandars).
Mary II, Letters of (Quarterly Review. Vol. 214).
Mary II (Nellie M. Waterson).
Mary, Life of Queen (Kathleen Woodward).
Mary, Princess (M. C. Carey).
Montagu, Letters of Lady Mary Wortley.
Netherland Historian, The (1675) (Stephen Swart).
Nicolas Papers, The (Camden Society).
Norfolk and Norwich Archæological Society, Original
    Papers of the.
Paston Letters.
Pepys's Diary.
Raikes's Journal.
Regal Records (J. R. Planché).
Regality, The Glory of (A. Taylor).
Regency, Memoirs of the (Duke of Buckingham).
Register, Annual.
Relics of Royalty (Joseph Taylor).
Romilly, Memoirs of the Life of Sir Samuel (By Him-
    self).
Royal and Illustrious Ládies, Letters of (M. A. E.
    Wood (Mrs. Everett Green)).
Rushworth's Collections.

Sermon (J. Leech).

Sidney Papers.

Stuart Princesses, Five (Robert S. Rait).

Stuarts, Memoirs Concerning the (J. Heneage Jesse).

Temple, Memoirs of Sir William.

Thurloe Papers.

Times, The.

Tudor Princesses, Lives of the (Agnes Strickland).

Verney Family, Memoirs of the (Margaret Verney).

Victoria, Queen (Sidney Lee).

Walpole, Letters of Horace (Ed. by Peter Cunning-
ham).

Wilberforce, Life of William (By his sons).

William, King, and Queen Mary, Conquerors (C.
Blount).

William, Prince of Orange (Marjorie Bowen).

William III, Court of (Edwin and Marion Sharpe Grew).

William IV and Victoria, Courts and Cabinets of (Duke
of Buckingham).

Winwood's Memorials.

Witte, The Administration of John de (Geddes).

York, Anne Hyde, Duchess of (J. R. Henslowe).

INDEX

242

down," 36 ; indignation at losing Mary Tudor, 59 ; engaged to Infanta, 67 ; agrees to marry Princess Mary, 67 ; supports Katharine of Aragon, 81 ; suggested as bridegroom, 94 ; diplomatic tension, 102

Charlotte, Queen, 209, 211, 213, 215

Chesterfield, Lord, 196

Clarence, Duke of, 210, 214–15

Clarendon, see Hyde

Claudia, Queen, 52

Cleves, Anne of, 90–1

Cleves, Duke of, 90

Cranmer, Archbishop of Canterbury, 114

Craven, Lord, writes to Elizabeth of Bohemia, 164

Cromwell, Thomas Lord, 85

Cromwell, Oliver, 144 ; rumour of his death, 151 ; threats to Holland, 154 ; death, 158

Cromwell, Richard, 158

D'Arblay, Madam, see Burney

Dauphins of France, 23, 65

Delany, Mrs., 213

Denmark, Kings of, 23, 204

Dorislaus, Dr. (Parliamentary agent), 146

Edward I, 12, 14, 15

Edward II, 15

Edward III, 16, 19, 20

Edward VI, 89, 92, 94 ; brides suggested, 95 ; journal entries, 100 ; his " devise," 102 ; death, 103 ; funeral services, 107

Eleanor of Provence, 11

Elizabeth (later Queen), offered to France, 83 ; out of favour, 87 ; under Katharine Parr, 93 ; named as inheritor of crown, 94 ; acquires worldly wisdom, 97 ; plot to place her on throne, 114 ; ascends, 117

Elizabeth (daughter of Charles I), 129, 130, 140, 142, 150

Elizabeth of Bohemia, 140, 151, 161

Elizabeth of York, 22, 23, 27

Emanuel (of Portugal), 28

Eustace, Prince, 5

Farmer, Richard, 92

Field of the Cloth of Gold, 67, 68

Fortescue, Sir Adrian, 67

Francis of Valois, see Valois

Frederick Henry, Prince, 135

Frederick, Prince of Wales, 197

Frederick of Hesse-Cassel, 197, 198, 203, 204

Funeral sermon on Mary Stuart, 124–5

Garneys, Sir Christopher, carries Mary Tudor to shore, 41

George II, 197, 198, 199, 202

George III, 209, 210–11, 215

George IV (as Prince), 209

George V, 225, 233

Gloucester, Bishop of, funeral sermon on Mary II, 190–1

Gloucester, Henry, Duke of, 150, 161, 162

Gloucester, William, Duke of, meets Mary (daughter of George III), 214 ; marriage, 216–18 ; establishment, 218 ; death, 220

Grey, Lady Jane, 95, 96, 103, 104, 105, 111

Guildford, Lady, 27, 43

Henrietta Maria, 129, 132, 133, 135 ; wishes to go abroad, 138–9 ; embarks, 140 ; sells her jewels, 141 ; a refugee, 152 ; her schemes, 155

Henry VII, 28, 29, 30, 33

Henry VIII, becomes King, 33 ; his rage, 35 ; accepts Louis XII of France for

DATE DUE

GAYLORD			PRINTED IN U.S A.